The Emancipation of Slaves Through Music

(Second Edition)

Mathew Knowles, MBA, Ph.D.

With Ashleigh M. Vernon, Bobby Browder Jr., Josie Deese, Richard Batiste, Vernecia Henry, Emerson Geter, Kye Williams, Phenicia Jones, Tashida Philan, and Timothy King

Copyright © 2021
Music World Publishing
PO Box 3727
Houston, TX 77253

Visit MathewKnowles.com to learn more!

All rights reserved, all pictures from Creative Commons,
Wiki Images, Public Domain
ISBN: 0692175776
ISBN-13: 978-0692175774

Plantation Dance, South Carolina circa 1790 featuring banjo and calabash. Image #NW0159 courtesy of the Virginia Foundation for the Humanities.

CONTENTS

	Introduction & Acknowledgments	5
1	Under the Yoke: One Voice	21
2	Follow That Banjo!	67
3	Message in the Music	93
4	Capturing the Truth	153
5	Who Wears the Mask?	173
6	Syncopations & Innovations	209
7	Beats, Revolution & Resistance	223
8	The Billion-Dollar Keys	231

INTRODUCTION

If you were suffering right now, could you sing or dance your way through it? When you feel captive to circumstances beyond your control, does music affect how you feel? For many, the rhythmic sounds of anything—a hum, a chant, a rap, some blues, a hymn, or just a good beat—is a form of medicine. For people suffering in the worst of times, art and music helped set their spirits—if not their bodies—free.

One might ask what makes a person feel captive to something these days? Even chained to our desks, toiling through long commutes, anguishing over finances or difficult coworkers or dysfunctional families, are we oppressed by these things? Perhaps once your outlook stretches into the racially charged, economic, socio-political, gender/cultural awareness, and civilian rights movements happening all around us, you find the real (metaphorical) chains that bind.

Human rights, employment opportunities, social advancement, community peace—all issues facing a suppressed part of society, made up of members who feel imprisoned by poverty, racism, sexism, violence, xenophobia, and more. In every country on the planet, a history of struggle can be found among some portion of people enslaved to an oppressive system. For many cultures still enduring centuries-long conflicts and war, it is their art that survives generations and sees them through the pain. It has been the resistance music that got them on their feet, the dances that made them bolder and stronger, the art that gave them an outlet for expression and voice.

This has been an especially unique journey for Africans, African Americans, Negros, Coloreds, Blacks, Afro-Latinx, Latinx, and so on. Names covering a people and their offspring over many eras but coming from one source: the transatlantic slave trade between Africa, the Caribbean, and North America. With the African people arrived a tremendous amount of cultural pride, craftsmanship, established faiths, talents, and skills. That they were stolen, traded, or sold before they took that transatlantic trip meant they transported a great deal of misery with them as well.

The gifts of art and culture, which could not be killed or cast overboard on the journey, became the African captives' tools for survival. The art forms of music, dance, and chant/rap/spoken-word in its earliest form were not used as weapons to emancipate the people by force all at once, but they helped them chisel out a unified voice. As the voices grew stronger and gained outside support, so did their numbers and spiritual capacity to fight and grow. As tools, they became codes and maps as well as musical messages used as keys to unlock both metaphorical and physical chains.

Bringing with these people their own culture, entertainment, religions, and expressions has caused a transformation in art around the world. Inside these pages, we examine how enslaved Africans brought with them, and passed down to us, an undefeatable instrument—our art forms, with a particular emphasis on music.

Yet for every song, there's a dance, along with the instruments that build and underpin the music which are also covered here. The influences keep stretching on, into the food we eat when dancing to good music and gathering like many Black families, such as mine, did on Sundays with fish fries, potlucks, and BBQs backed by loud music and laughter. Where did it come from?

Line-dancing to a Frankie Beverly and Maze song at a soul food Sunday dinner or cookout in the Black community is deeply ingrained in some of us in this generation. Here, we'll find it goes back generations with a deeper, special meaning. Music wasn't just a tool for joyous gatherings and dancing in good spirit; it was a powerful outlet needed in more serious conditions. It was once as controlled and suppressed as the people, as with the outlawing of drum playing on plantations during slavery.

Why would a natural God-given gift be so brutally silenced by Western imperialists if it was not so powerful? If one wonders why music wasn't potent enough to free the captives bodily, by the end of these pages perhaps you will see all the ways it did. These were people in chains possessing no bows, arrows, spears nor guns to assist in their emancipation. And, yet, the persistence and even the insistence of their culture—in everything from food, art, and invention to music—fought for them. The art gave them a voice and a distinct presence in society. As their art grew bolder and spread, so did their voices. And as their voices drew strength in unity, their bodies lined up together as a force for change.

Incrementally, these captives and their descendants worked the locks on the heaviest chains, and music chronicled these stages. This generation is still picking the locks on other issues that bind us, and we too have a soundtrack to our emancipation. You can trace every socio-political battle and civil rights action that worked those chains loose and find music as their backbeat. The voices in unison (calling and answering, "What do we want?" "Freedom now!") at a rally, march, protest, gathering, or in an anthem galvanized them beyond the speeches. A drum roll leading a march or voices in unity during a protest were examples of that backbeat.

By examining the roots and evolution of modern music, dance, and even Black comedy, we see all developed from the same sources and understand how far it has traveled and why. Following the sounds—from instruments such as the modern banjo (and its native African origins) to the drum, on into rap beats, reggae dancehall music, and even breakdancing—we will better understand the power of the journey.

Music has been at the foundation of every aspect of my career as an industry executive, artist manager, and university professor for over thirty years. Yet a deep exploration of its influence didn't come until my Special Topics class, where I asked my Texas Southern University students, "In what ways did music emancipate the spirits of enslaved people? In what ways does it liberate people today?" Their research, resources, and contributions on the subject became the basis for this book.

What the collective assessment of music created from the slave era until now has shown us is that long before an official Emancipation Proclamation was made, enslaved people had found other ways to free—if not their physical bodies from chains—their spirits. When a spirit is free, no earthly ideas (such as slavery) can bind you, and your energy is not spent on being a better captive but rather gaining and enjoying freedom. Once the mind tastes freedom, the body will fight to follow. You will fight for that right in whatever ways you know how. That strong spirit forges tremendous willpower, and that changes society when applied. We can use music today for the same spiritually empowering effects.

The musical style passed down to us taught us that through the pain, desire to be heard could always be expressed with the art. Even the birth of a child, a wedding, or a talk with God were emotional moments the slaveholders could not suppress inside a captive. If the love of a newborn child stirred someone enough to dance or sing in celebration, it was a natural expression that arose in them, one uncontrolled by the so-called masters. The death of a loved one, brutal treatment by a foreman, or the pain of slavery, period, could also bring out insuppressible wails, shouts, or moans. That a moan could then become a melody, and ultimately inform the music later called the blues, proves the unstoppable spirit of music in man.

The music we love today would never have existed had Africans not touched these shores. The end of the road in this study leaves us with a final important question that only the individual reader can answer for themselves: How does that music they left us liberate you today?

Does a choir on Sunday morning or your grandma's soft hum soothe your soul? Does a hard drumbeat or a slick guitar lick make you want to get up and move? Does a mind-stirring rap or gospel song make you stop and think? Do you feel spaceless when you're inside a good song, as if nothing can reach you there? Those questions answered with "yes" prove the power of music for anybody.

Whatever music does for you when you are in your hardest moments is what will affect how much you relate to the people who were literally enslaved. We describe their conditions here because maybe the roots of grandma's hum are inherited from a place of pain this generation cannot relate to—even with all our current oppressions.

When we investigate the origins of African art, we'll see the people, their trials and triumphs, and their fingerprints all over what we know as modern entertainment. The music passed down from African slaves has redefined Western entertainment as we know it, even while it has been suppressed, discriminated against, appropriated, and sharecropped since it started being a money-making commodity.

Behind that music, we discover a remarkable people. On this subject, please note throughout your read how each term used here to describe the people changes with each era. For example, when describing the African captives who were considered slaves, we say "captives" because that is what they were. They were only slaves on paper to some slave owner. I dislike referring to men and women themselves as slaves throughout the book as if that is their designated race (exceptions are where quoting another reference or for clarity).

In the eras to follow for the next generations, society no longer called them Africans, as they were first-generation descendants. Instead, they were called Negro (or its ugly derivatives), Colored, and then Black by the 1950s-'70s on, when I was coming up. As eras and locations change, so might the reference to the individuals being discussed here. They were Africans held captive. Their children were Americans born of Africans. The other titles morphed with the times, and I'm not one to pick and choose if it fits the era because I want to really take you there.

While the people's names changed, along with their status, the culture and influences from their homeland were persistent. The songs we know and the growth of modern music into rock, rap, gospel, country, and R&B, etc., trace not just to the coasts of the Motherland but to the ships bringing the people from it by force. They were forced to surrender many of their traditions, sometimes their voices, and quite often their lives; it is a wonder their music survived at all. The fact that their descendants today can rap about oppression for millions of dollars is a miracle by itself. The power of song proved itself as one of few things that could not be chained up, shut up, or killed.

Even with our ignorance of its history, some inner understanding about these captives' traumas informs today's art. The oppression and racism amplified by slavery are still real, and you can hear their effects echoing through every note of Black music today. The generations coming up now still deal with issues related to slavery's aftermath. If you listen to music with this history in mind, perhaps you will hear the influences that remain.

When I was a boy, music in my house was as fundamental to our lives as food. The two often went well together. My job was essentially acting as a DJ for our household dance parties. I kept coins of various denominations ready to place on top of the needle to weigh it down over the record's scratches, thus keeping the vibe going unstopped. If I could, I would take some of the first 78 RPM records, add music from my era into this generation, and DJ this story. (I will leave you with recommended listening as well as reading to mark each era.)

Because from one music lover to another, it is time we retrace those lines since the truth itself sets us free. Knowing the long and storied journey of it will peel back every song you listen to, and I promise you won't hear them the same way again.

Mathew Knowles, Houston, TX - June 2018

ACKNOWLEDGMENTS

Special thanks to the exhaustive research and writing assignments of the following Entertainment and Recording Industry Management degree program students at Texas Southern University. From their quest, I could gather the history alongside these students' modern perspectives in this musical examination. I appreciate their ideas and dialogue that greatly added to this collection. Much appreciation to: Ashleigh M. Vernon, Bobby Browder Jr., Josie Deese, Richard Batiste, Vernecia Henry, Emerson Geter, Kye Williams, Phenicia Jones, Tashida Philan, and Timothy King.

"... And so, by fateful chance the Negro folk song—the rhythmic cry of the slave—stands today not simply as the sole American music, but as the most beautiful expression of human experience born this side of the seas."

—W. E. B. Du Bois

CHAPTER ONE

UNDER THE YOKE: ONE VOICE

Let's just get the facts upfront: The amount of destruction slavery brought on the African people is proportionate to how much recovery its descendants still face to this day.

"The slave trade deprived the African continent of some of its healthiest and most skilled men and women. The enslaved Africans were transported mainly from West Africa to South and North America. The trade occurred through what was known as the triangular trade route and Middle Passage. During the period that the trade lasted, which is believed to have been between 1526 to 1867, more than 12.5 million slaves were transported from Africa. In human history, the transatlantic slave trade was probably the most expensive, cold-hearted, and insensitive of all of the long-distance global migrations." *(Eltis & Engerman, 1993)*

As ugly as it was, the slave trade had a tremendous influence on the beautification of American art. Would musical forms such as blues, gospel, and jazz have been developed without it? Research suggests not. One must admire music for what it has accomplished in this way. Just as we admire the many genres added from Caribbean and South American African cultures, like reggae and salsa. That sound was first taken from a land rich with instruments, dance, and vocal celebration. Fortunately, it didn't die with the slave era or under its terrible yoke.

Stripped from its roots in Africa where it celebrated and communicated life, the continent's art, people, and culture transformed America for over 400 years. Even torn from their tribes and forced among strangers in a new land, the people would learn not only how to unite using their voices but how to tuck meaning behind everything from a hum to a hymn. In tracing the pain of slavery, we find the tools they used, including music as ever-healing, melodic medicine.

Slavery was not just forced labor; it was a slow form of genocide that both the people and the music managed to mostly survive. While seemingly removing what looks like enslavement "from the books," we now have the privately owned prison industrial complex, which houses as many young Black men as slaveholders ever did—not to overlook the modern examples of sharecropping bordering on slavery in the corporate world (even in the music business).

Always, music and art is a guide to what continued to happen to African people from the traumatic transatlantic trip all the way through the racial battles in America for centuries after. As we uncover what has been buried, partially erased, or denied credit, unfortunately, we must wade through some troubled waters.

Making money from cheap labor became a driving motivation and helped fuel the rise of slavery throughout the seventeenth century. It only took the realization in colonial Virginia that tobacco was queen to cotton's king for the 1620s and 1630s to find the establishing of a colony of settlers with imported, poor Englishmen as its primary labor. Due to decline in the price of tobacco, a third of the English population dying off due to the Great Plague, and a devastating fire in London, employment options opened for English laborers at home, and the number of immigrants to the New World shrank as fast as it had started.

With Native Americans prone to diseases carried by foreigners, not to mention all the continued rebellions, Africans proved to be a better replacement for those early colonizers. This left remaining colonizers free to quickly set up active trade, enslaving Africans against their will—and more easily—by taking them far from home.

While the slave trade had been happening in Europe since Portugal's fifteenth-century exploration of the African coast, it became a booming commodity once the New World took it in. The preservation of music, dance, and culture started along the transatlantic journey itself as a means for captives' surviving the journey, yet it continued to grow after their arrival. Art and music are so woven into their survival that as we observe their horrendous journey, we get to watch the art forms also evolve.

Here before you is a jukebox from the era when ships started arriving and shortly thereafter. I don't have the records to spin for you like I did when I was a kid, but I can describe it for you. You see, most of the music influencing early America was what was coming out of New England, and that was mostly hymns. Those religious tunes shaped society, along with Puritans, who introduced their own style of church hymns when they arrived.

What secular music there was tended to be Broadside Ballads and British folk, alongside classical favorites that live today. Many of the religious order frowned on instruments, so their music would have been lean on rhythms with an organ at most—and even that was controversial.

This sounds sleepy by way of dance music, so let's spice it up. Historian Edgar McManus explained how the colonies could not have survived without slave labor and how that labor transformed this land. What McManus said of the labor, we will say of the art forms lacking the African presence—sleepy. Just like European food before introduction to other countries' exotic spices, the songs were primarily flavorless—especially if you were not a religious Puritan. The taste of the music would be bland compared to anything we have today. You damn sure couldn't dance to it. Basically, it lacked a beat.

Beats are best delivered by drums and, until the African population introduced the variety of drums and techniques for playing, any drumming sounds came with military and funeral marches. Whether the society of highly religious colonists knew it or not, they were about to import a spice in the form of music, that would be better-tasting food for the soul.

During that era, except for precious metals, African people became the primary export to Europe and eventually the New World. Also dubbed "the triangular trade" because it connected the economies of three continents—Europe, Africa, and America—this saw millions of human beings forcibly deported from their homes and enslaved by those heinous trading systems. The figure of a million African enslaved lives excludes those who died aboard the ships during transportation between the continents.

The triangle of trade spread to all the countries' colonies and outposts, as the world was expanding and exploring new territories to conquer. This led to what is known as the African diaspora, which refers to the spread of its people and culture throughout the world—including the Caribbean, South and North America, Africa, and Europe. The only means of transport were massive cargo holding ships that could stack tens of hundreds of men, women, and children like logs and haul them to various ports around the world, where enslavers waited to buy them.

The options for escaping a ship crowded in filth and misery were few for those held on them, drowning or starving themselves were the main two—that is, for those who didn't die from the conditions themselves or from murder at the hands of captors for any minor infraction. Being that each slave had a price tag on them, some owners of the ships wouldn't allow them to starve and would force feed them.

The odors from dead bodies, excretions, and vomit due to seasickness filled the air along with their cries. Not only did the captives endure physical torture, they had psychological torment to deal with as well. Homesickness and uncertainty about any sort of future added to the trauma. Again, if you were in such pain (you, the reader), could you manage to sing?

Even speaking different languages, torn from a variety of tribes and separate regions, the one thing they could depend on was their understanding of music to both communicate emotion and express feelings. Sounds in the dank hole might have begun as a loud moan or a low whimper that would signal distress but escalate into spiritual calls for mercy and divine intervention. The sounds of African Muslims in prayer and supplication would have brought an emotional song with it. Lullaby-type songs from their native lands were sung to console the children and eventually others on the ship responded to the sound as well.

This opened a new level of awareness of one another, despite the language and tribal differences. They could bridge the barrier using something as easily learned or mimicked as a song. They soon realized music could also serve in sending a message and, therefore, help in planning acts of rebellion on the ship. Even the rattling of chains binding them became instruments or messages. Not mere melodies and noises, these became war room schemes for "how do we get out of this alive?"

One of the last men aboard one of those ships will finally have his story told, eighty-seven years after writer/anthropologist Zora Neale Hurston interviewed Cudjoe Lewis in 1927 for the Journal of Negro History. She also made a short film about Lewis. Finally, after she refused to change the dialect that most authentically reflected its character over eighty years ago, her book was released. Barracoon: The Story of the Last "Black Cargo" was Hurston's posthumously published, annotated edition, in May 2018. A recent discovery of what might be one of the last (illegal but active anyway) transatlantic slave ships, the Clotilda, off the shores of Mobile, Alabama. There it dropped off between 110 to 120 Africans in 1860, fifty-two years after America had abolished the international slave trade.

In a rare event at the end of the Civil War, African captives were left alone to fend for themselves. This led them to forge out a thriving, self-sustaining community in Mobile called Africa Town. It held on to all its languages, music, dance, and art as well as its religious and tribal customs. Each of them retained full memory of their homeland and passed it down generations. Today, the town is a local legend, and the story behind it is by itself a fascinating study.

Joseph Lewis, among the first generation born in America, learned how to read alongside other children from lessons taught at the church the settlers founded. This aided in the preservation of his father Cudjoe's story of the happenings aboard the Clotilda. Before he died, his father was recorded on film as the last living example of the people brought directly to these shores and enslaved.

Cudjoe Lewis, as an unbroken link to his African Yoruba people, provides a glimpse at what the captives left behind, such as the family sizes and sense of community among the tribes. He was the second of four children with twelve stepsiblings, living in the Banté region of eastern Benin. Born with the name Kossola, he was the grandson of an officer of the region's king, and by age fourteen he too was training to be a soldier.

A look at the types of skills in which he was trained gives us another look at the abilities these men, women, and even young children had before they were enslaved. They brought considerable knowledge from home of agriculture, farming, herb and medicine cultivation, and food preparation, even in times of famine—all to serve colonists who took a century just to learn how to not starve in America.

By the time Cudjoe Lewis and other captives arrived, he knew how to track game in a hunt, fight like a soldier, and use weapons from spears to arrows and more. He could defend his home as well as any man. He was even inducted into his tribe's secret Yoruban society, which acted as a policing force behind the tribe's order, called the Oro. Still, he and others were sold after being attacked by another African tribe, the Dahomey, in April 1860. After murdering the king, the Dahomey invaders took Lewis and others to cage-like slave pens. They were then taken to the coast, where they were held for three weeks in barracoons (thus the title of Hurston's book), before being shipped away.

From as far as Nigeria, other captives were gathered aboard the Clotilda, where Lewis (then known as Kossola) was dragged aboard naked. When emancipation took place in 1865, he obtained freedom and kept the name Lewis. A woman who had also been aboard the ship became his wife, and their lives continued along the coasts of Mobile, Alabama, so far from home. Yet those varying tribes formed a common ground in Africa Town and their music and art merged, much as it must have done when they were first trying to communicate together on the ship.

In *"Legacies of Slavery: Dance,"* Dr. Alan Rice writes about the disconnect between the varying tribes on slave ships due to the lack of common language. Naturally, music, being a universal element, could fill the gaps where words could not. Dance and song were things anyone could pick up on quickly, and once they realized these modes could communicate ideas, they used them often.

When forced to dance for their daily exercise upon the ship's decks as the only time for air or sunshine out of the stinking hole, that alone might have been a reason to sing in relief. Yet it was not time wasted, as the men and women took this chance to use dances and religious chants to form solidarity and strengthen their bodies for possible insurrection.

Modern dances such as the limbo in the Caribbean are a good example of what carried over from those ships based on the limited space they had and their attempts to escape it. Rice also writes about the dance—the cakewalk—evolving at that time from slaves making fun or mocking the enslaving colonizers on the sly. Even movement could be an active protest in dance.

Negro spirituals—more aptly called "sorrow songs"—were created once the Africans were exposed (often by force) to Christianity. The emotional and solemn nature of the tunes expressed the deep sorrow of their conditions and longings for home and freedom. The spiritual aspects of their songs, pre-Christianity, would have been reflective of African tribal religions and Islam.

The religions the tribes came with are important in how music and art were shaped during slavery. Gathered evidence from slaveholders' letters and documents indicate there were many imported African Muslims. As early as the Revolutionary War in 1775, Muslims fought alongside Americans in the military.

America has no record of ever being without Muslims in its population. While most of the enslaved people came with traditional tribal customs, including ancestor worship, animism (the belief that everything—including rocks, animals, and plants—has spirits) and other religious practices, at least 30 percent or more (as many were forced to hide their beliefs to survive and may be unrecorded) were Muslims. The very meat of the US Constitution is freedom of religion, which meant there had to be more than one variety running around.

In Virginia, Thomas Jefferson not only owned a copy of the Qur'an, he wrote treatises that called for inclusive religious freedoms, including those of Muslims and Jews. It was amended before Ratification; forefathers of the Constitution eventually took out non-Christian groups, yet the fact that they were acknowledged shows their small but recognizable numbers.

African Muslims' faith met challenges and scrutiny as they struggled to maintain traditional practices. They often found a disagreeable welcome in the form of both legal and social acceptance.

"I knew several [people] who must have been, from what I have since learned, Mohamedans [Muslims]; though at that time, I had never heard of the religion of Mohamed. There was one man on this plantation ... who prayed five times every day, always turning his face to the east, when in the performance of his devotion."

—Charles Ball, 1837

Literate, bilingual, and highly ritualized in their practices, African Muslims in America left written documentation of their journey, usually in Arabic. They also used their language to secretly communicate with one another, as shown by letters of exchange. Their autobiographical journals, recorded in diaries and sometimes even love letters, paint a picture of their lives. Asked by slaveholders to write in Arabic scriptures from the Bible, some African captives wrote verses from the Qur'an denouncing slavery, with the slaveholder completely unaware of the true meaning.

While intelligent, skilled, and faithful, African Muslims suffered were forced to adopt what would be to them sacrilegious rules, whether in dress, diet, or restrictions to their traditional fasts and prayer times.

Those transported Muslims, like many of the Caribbean Christian converts, found ways to cloak their faith inside their conversions. Called "Taqiyyah" [Tak-e-ya] in Islam, the term means permissible silence or denial of religious practice under persecution, which the Islamic faith had to adopt when forced to convert as captives or in conflict. Nevertheless, small practices were tucked away in simple everyday life and subtle nods to Islam's Five Pillars, such as traditional feast foods and freewill offering.

To protect their lives and their families, some cloaked their faith as a tool for freedom. One enslaved African pretended to be Christian in order to use the American Colonization Society to gain sponsorship back to Africa (no doubt unbeknownst to his benefactors). Others in history, like Ayuba Suleiman Diallo, remained stubbornly faithful to Islam, to the extent he won over his slaveholder, who then freed him and sent him back to the continent in style. Most of the others just suffered or converted until the Islamic faith was all but diminished on plantations in America.

The music and art remained as they were absorbed into the daily lives of the captives, such as the practice called ring shouting, a circle of people clapping, shouting, singing, and foot shuffling in a rotating counterclockwise motion. Ring shouting was emerged in places like the Georgia Sea Islands, where enslaved African Muslims like Salih Bilali copied traditional Mecca pilgrimage habits of circling the Kaaba in dance circles. Another remnant is the music, particularly tracing primitive blues music origins to Islamic prayer sounds and tonation. These started with passed-down styles derived from adhan (ad'hän), the Islamic call to prayer — where riveting vocalizations draw deeply emotional and melodic tones.

So, with a slave import population of up to 30 percent Muslims, Islam brought its own rich music and culture to the mix, having long established itself on the West African coast. Christianity was something the people learned to incorporate into their own customs that would not be erased, even with force. Many reestablished their religious beliefs but kept the use of music as a spiritual expression, unique to their experiences.

The author of The Talking Book, Allen Dwight Callahan, offers more excellent reading on this subject. His research helped me understand that the Muslims who arrived were already familiar with their own holy book. Having been taught to both read and write, they had an easier transition in converting to the religious tenets of the Bible. However, those who could not read or write and came with other traditional African worship rituals had the challenge of understanding the white man's religion.

Music bridged the gap as a way for the oral lessons from the Bible they were being taught (but couldn't read or write) to be memorized. The African storytelling tradition was used to help communicate their understanding in familiar ways. Thus, negro spirituals, which borrowed biblical references and merged them with musical delivery, came about naturally when flavorless hymns met the beat behind a plaintive African's plea.

Although enslaved Muslims and other African tribal members eventually converted to Christianity (even if just to keep peace and stay alive), there were those thinkers, like Frederick Douglass, who resisted the idea of feeding those people still in slavery more of it. The idea of sending Bibles to them, particularly in the south, was one he and others opposed initially. Even though he had been illiterate himself until adulthood, he still had a head full of Bible by the time he was free.

He recalled verbatim the lessons from the Bible he was given orally by his slaveholders. In many of those lessons, the scriptures selected emphasized the obedient roles of slaves and their submission. The way it was delivered, it reinforced the notion that holding the Africans and their offspring captive was a God-given right and a charitable deed as well. Knowing the southern slaves were being indoctrinated by those lessons, Douglass felt it added to their inability to adopt the willpower to free themselves, especially if they had been told it was God's own will that made them captives. He thought it would be better for them not to have that book at all.

But by the Second Great Awakening, Methodists and Baptists were everywhere, including among slave populations that had formerly held Muslim and African tribal worshippers. The conversion complete, people merged willingly or in secret alliance to their own behind their slaveholders' backs. They found common ground and made it work, such as in the act of baptism by water, which was similar to traditions with streams and water rituals done in Africa. With such similarities, it was easier for them to adapt to the newness.

Literacy factored greatly in how the Bible was absorbed into the culture, being that most of it was orally preached and sung in hymns and psalms. Callahan describes the process of "lining" a song or a hymn, where the leader tosses out the first line of the song and the others would sing it back.

Singing the words became an easier way to deliver them to the congregation who, in repeating them back, were performing the act of memorization and absorption. That repetitive exchange pattern is one modern preachers continue to employ. If any of you had a grandmother or great-grandmother who "couldn't read nor write but knew every word of the Bible," this miracle was performed in just that way.

The Great Awakening, when American Christianity began to expand its doctrines and converts such as the Baptist and Methodist churches, swelled membership into tens of thousands by 1813. Even as abolitionists pushed for freedom, slaveholders rounded up an "apostle to the Negro slave" and took to evangelizing as many of them as they could reach throughout the south and the happy slaves who served them in an attempt to show a kinder, gentler Christian slaveholder—under a God who sanctioned it.

When the weary workers would finally convene in some "camp meet" or even grouped in the field, the preaching they got and the music they sang had its own effects. Regardless of how the white Christians tried to lead them to the Holy Spirit, their traditional methods of devotion brought them the "Good News" gospel in a way the Puritans could never know. What the people got instead was a transcendental experience that struck them with the "Holy Ghost," and in their own way they used it to redeem their lives from the hands of earthly oppression.

This self-styled approach to worship allowed them to connect personally with God. No matter their former faith, they could derive comfort from the beliefs they now practiced and their unique ways of delivering and absorbing it all, from Bible lessons to hymns. Worship gave them secret keys to unlocking what all the fuss was about—their souls.

Even if abolitionists, Puritans, and missionaries genuinely cared about the salvation of African captives, they could only offer the religion; they couldn't reach inside an enslaved man with mere words. Any true conversion, even after the "Good News" slanted in slaveholders' favor with facts such as Africans having been cursed since the time of Noah, came from their own emotional connections.

The ingrained, generational habits of worship they arrived with, as well as music, drumming, dress, and food, all played a part in how they celebrated a higher power.

Some of the rituals of Christianity, like baptism by water, would have been familiar to them and easy to conform to. Others, especially anything enforcing the ideas behind their enslavement, must have been difficult to swallow. The only hope they could create would be in promises the scriptures made. The act of going inside while riding the waves of an emotionally penetrating song, concentrating on a higher source, allows for a moment the ability to leave your surroundings. This was a meditation that, for as long as it lasted, felt like freedom.

Did Christianity stop the captives' desire to revolt? Did the "slaves obey your masters" teachings work by encouraging submission? These were questions Fredrick Douglass and his contemporaries had when facing the continued advancement of Negro evangelical leaders should their passed-down sermons and interpretations be unknowing tools for slavery and inequality.

It's a catch-22 in some ways. The traditionally faith-filled people were suddenly deprived of any method of worship until handed the acceptable Christian doctrine, as flavored by the white population enslaving them. It was useful for keeping the peace and, as we'll see later, in hiding their true intentions when needed. It was habit to take what tools they were given and make better ones or instruments from the spare parts; they took foods like hog guts and feet and made meals southern folks call "soul food" today. The religion and its songs when they came to them may have been dry and meant to hold them down, but African spices and colors, as with all things, changed that.

Negro spirituals occurred as a combination of traditional African music with Christian-European hymns, with the songs addressing the hardships they had to endure. When used as codes, which we'll get deeper into here, the songs safely used names or areas such as rivers or mountains that were biblical in context to symbolize different aspects of their lives. This was significant for convincing slaveholders of their conversion to the Bible over the Qur'an or ancient ancestor-based tribal religions. Still, the continued connection of the rhythms and beats that were traditional to them allowed a memory of their homeland to remain.

Interestingly, Christianity was not handed to the captives willingly at first. The religion and, subsequently, the church, out of which we derive the heart and soul of Black music, and most every other American music genre, also grew out of struggle.

These were not savages, nor pagans or atheists, that needed a good dose of Christ when they got to America. They already had an upbringing of some type of faith. Imagine having that all your life until someone forced it from you. For example, drums were an integral part of African life. The beats spoke words and traveled as messengers from region to region, and they made ceremonies and rituals complete. Once that was known by slaveholders in America, drums were strictly outlawed.

Having their traditional drums, forms of worship, and even language stripped away, the improvisations they used to hold on to their cultural arts were outright ingenious. European enslavers deprived African captives of material possessions, yet despite the restrictions, survivors recreated variations on familiar instruments with what they had on hand.

When resources were not available, slaves were innovative and created new instruments from the materials that were around. Objects found in environments throughout the Americas and Caribbean show they were literate, bilingual, and highly ritualized in their practices. African Muslims in America left written documentation of their journeys, usually in Arabic. They also used their language to secretly communicate with one another, as shown by letters of exchange. Their autobiographical journals, recorded in diaries and sometimes even love letters, paint a picture of their lives.

Asked by slaveholders to write in Arabic scriptures from the Bible, some African captives wrote verses from the Qur'an denouncing slavery, with the slaveholder completely unaware of the true meaning. While intelligent, skilled, and faithful, African Muslims suffered while forced to adopt what would be to them sacrilegious rules, whether in dress, diet, or restrictions to their traditional fasts and prayer times.

Those transported Muslims, like many of the Caribbean Christian converts, found ways to cloak their faith inside their conversions.

Like the modern drum, one can easily see that the guitar and banjo's origins also came from these African innovations. Some of the intricate ways American banjos are still being designed gives us a look at the survival of the African tradition.

During their free time, slaves constructed drums, fiddles, rattles, bells, and stringed instruments that resemble the guitar and banjo. Along with the creation of instruments, slaves also developed new forms of music reflective of the environment and the conditions that they endured while still preserving their African heritage.

The genres of music created were indicative of the location of the people, and the songs were often composed spontaneously by the entire community. In the Caribbean and Latin America, new genres of music such as calypso, soca, rumba, and samba all developed. Elsewhere, forms like bachata came courtesy of the Dominican Republic as a blend of both African and Spanish influences and often conveyed sadness or heartbreak.

Remembering that the limbo dances were exercise tools and physical training aboard slave ships, one can question the beginnings of all other moves that accompanied music in these places. Dance—like the instruments, vibrantly dyed fabrics, foods, and art—is fundamentally a branch that grows up from music's roots. African music inspires active participation, and its beauty calls for likewise expressions.

To have had that limited or stifled must have been hell for people steeped in music and dance from birth. Among the oldest race on earth, the African Sān (called

Pygmies by colonizers) still dance today in a round circle that includes the infirm, the unhappy, the crying baby, and the old man on his last days—everyone dances.

If you're sick, they have a dance; you get married, there's another. They even now have one for when the white man harms one of their people. The movement accompanied every major event, just as the music did. To be forced to dance in chains so they would be fit to sell, or by choice to keep fit to rebel movement was crucial to a captive.

However, the effects of the African diaspora made for worldwide preservation of not just music and sound but movement and physical expression, despite slaveowners' efforts to suppress it. The Caribbean and New Orleans seaport captives were better able to keep hold of the traditional arts than, say, those in the American south, who were stripped of all but the barest aspects of humanity. In Jamaica, the music evolved with its own dance forms, such as the Afro-Caribbean "quadrille," and into festivities like a

"Junkanoo," a musical street parade with colorful costumes from the African Akan tribe. "Fancy dress" festivals were common among island people, reflected even in the carnivals of Brazil and other South American countries created by African-descended people.

Large, loud, colorful gatherings with music and lots of dancing, all energized by instruments like drums, marked these occasions: a taste of the homeland that survived and even thrived. Among those enslaved, celebrations were no doubt rare but necessary breaks from the toil of servitude. Starting in the twentieth century, Jamaican songs, like other music throughout the region, reflected that, as in tunes like Harry Belafonte's "Day-O (Banana Boat Song)," which copied work songs from laborers and became a mainstream hit.

Music provided rhythm for repetitive chores, such as working in the fields and on the docks or boats. Under the baking sun with a foreman at their backs, railroad tracks or crops stretching for miles at their feet, African women, children, and men worked daily. They developed rhythmic shouts and hollers as a melodic means of expression during this exertion. If you think about it, using rhythmic beats to back synchronized tasks such as working in teams was an excellent way to keep up the pace and timing.

With someone in the lead, a shouted call opened the conversation as others joined in a yelled response. The traditional beating of a drum would have been the backbeat to such labor on the continent of Africa; however, slaveholders forbade them from playing them. Chains, the sounds of picks hitting dirt, and shouts would have to do on plantations.

Apart from Louisiana, that is, where Catholic laws, unlike southern Protestant ideology, allowed drum playing in places like New Orleans. This being a major port for the slave trade in America for a long while, the use of drums gained a foothold in the music developed in that region, more so than anywhere else in America.

"In Louisiana during the eighteenth century, slaves were commonly allowed Sundays off from their work. They could gather in the 'Place de Negres,' informally 'Place Congo,' where the slaves would set up a market, sing, dance, and play music." — Peter Kolchin

It was the preservation of the culture and the instruments, particularly the drums, that led to the inevitable birth of jazz and laid the foundations for rock music. There was a specific sound the people there could create that was distinctly dominated by the variety of Caribbean, Native American, French European, and African music that mingled together in Congo Square during the height of slavery's era there. All the jazz and blues greats who grew up in New Orleans would have been heavily influenced by those sounds.

Once the Civil War was over, there were plenty of instruments to be salvaged from the military, and as a result, the snare drums, horns, and fifes filled the air. It made for a syncopated sound that reflected an exotic blend of every culture you could lay eyes on there. Ragtime and blues would have been the backbeat to barrooms and brothels, along with Salon and Afro-Latin music, quadrilles, marching bands, and more. It was a multi-lingual and blended racial mixture of people who, when harmonically linked together in their unique styles, created the origins of jazz.

For some, according to illustrations such as the one above, it started as more cacophony than symphony. Yet over time, as hybrids more easily blended into a simpler style with more simplistic arrangements, it was all the rage. From the drumbeats and distinct playing patterns, the sound that became rock was born there as well. Congo Square's music, including drums, was again an exception to the rule. What else would shake up a plantation more than the sound of such exotic force pounding?

Even if they didn't believe messages hid behind every drumming beat, they had to know the power it struck down in the memories and hearts of the African people, and even their descendants. Although removed by generations from their homeland, the drumbeat and its energy still held a motivating summons for the people. Once they found how a song could carry a secretly rebellious message through the air and rally others to join the fight, they began to pick the locks on those chains in America.

European classical music was enjoyed by wealthy aristocratic members of society who avoided rhythm and considered it not just lowly but a mark of the underclasses. It denied both the music of Africa and its people. The early absence of spice to classical European waltzes, operas, and hymns makes them distinct from the African rhythms that got mixed in later. Native American musical influences and the rustic folk sounds mixed into the earliest years of the slave era as well, and all of it influenced the developing sounds.

If the spread of the different styles is based on where the African people were placed, the distinct development of each genre of music would make sense. Some styles never influenced certain regions during slavery because of the tight control slaveholders enforced. For example, the South American Spanish slaveowners, after 800 years of Islamic dominance by North African Moors in Spain, didn't like the idea of bringing in Muslims as slaves. Those mostly Senegalese and Malian captives went to North American enslavers in America. The people from those regions of Africa brought the Islamic culture's musical influence, with string instruments and songs, while Nigerian/Congolese and Ghanaian peoples relied on traditional drumming styles that survive in music today.

Such an exotic sound, enhanced by the throbbing tones of the drum, is powerful, and was no doubt an intimidating element to those early colonists who were used to blander melodies. For a while, the more Africanized music might have existed unchecked. However, just as it had been used in the homeland, the drum was a voice that could signal between plantations and communicate more than mere words. Once the enslavers caught on, they had to stop it, unanimously.

"It is absolutely necessary to the safety of this Province, that all due care be taken to restrain Negroes from using or keeping of drums, which may call together or give

sign or notice to one another of their wicked designs and purposes."

— *Slave Code of South Carolina, Article 36 (1740)*

Yet the need to have that flavoring to their music was persistent, and with drums outlawed, people used everything at hand to get those desired beats—tabletops, spoons, and dishes, or basic foot stomping in a ring shout gathering like "patting juba," or beating on chests and limbs. Every soft shoe, tap dance, or foot shuffle that exists no doubt evolved out of those practices. Absent drums, shouts and hollers, chants, and cadences in the field would have to provide the backbeat. By suppressing the drum, American enslavers only ended up empowering the African people to recreate their traditional sounds in other ways; the results are what you hear today, tucked down in an undefeatable beat.

Though many regions were influenced by other nations, Sub-Saharan music remained self-contained. With its influence, we find literally hundreds of African songs that celebrate every event from marriage and childbirth to hunting party victories.

That is because music, particularly the drum, had specific uses, as did the dance. This use went as far as which instruments could or could not be used during ceremonies, and its travel to America did not change that.

Songs could be either celebrating an event, warding off evil spirits, or paying ancestor homage with a specific dance or ceremony accompanying it. These same dances are done today with little awareness of their true meanings as ceremonies. Just as with the dances, the ranking of importance and use with instruments included the idea of its spirit, even down to the very carvers who made it (especially true with drums) whose role in crafting

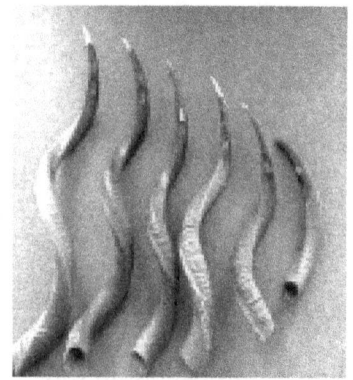

instruments was highly esteemed. Instruments influenced by different tribes were recreated to fit in with special rituals and customs, and the person who played the instrument was usually the one who crafted it.

    Their inventions in instrumentation and persistence in keeping them led to using gourds, metal and tin, wood, and bone just to render as close of a copy as possible to that kora or drum they had back home. Their craving for those sounds all led to the beats, rhythms, lyrics, melodies, and bars we now have. Without them, the voices would have echoed alone, without the resonance and beauty of the strings,

drums, flutes, and percussion. The wind instruments made of reeds, horns, conches, panpipes, tusks, bamboo, or metal piping also helped back storytelling with traditional sounds.

Percussion sounds were also created from wooden sticks and clay pots, bells and tambourines, and rain sticks from hollowed-out wood, with small pebbles moving vigorously inside.

Beyond its appeal to the listener, in African culture the instrument itself tells a story without being played. They are decorated and seen as works of art, with great pride being put into details such as symbolically sculpted figurines and messages. There is a reason they are covered with patterns and decorated with other accessories like beads and feathers or colorful paint and animal skin. They were spiritual tokens empowering the musician to filter godly or ancestral messages.

Nothing was going to stop the transmission of their natural rhythms, forms of praise, and need for the flavor of a beat. It had been the true path to inner freedom even before chains were introduced.

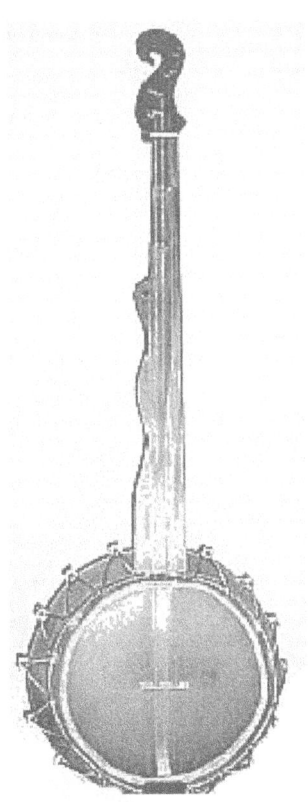

"One of the reasons country music was created by African Americans, as well as European Americans, is because Blacks and whites in rural communities in the south often worked and played together."

— DeFord Bailey

CHAPTER TWO

FOLLOW THAT BANJO!

When it comes to instruments that are based on African culture, we find they provide more than notes. They open a connection between the soul of the continent and its stolen people. The music is a conduit for never forgetting that bond. Such strength in heritage would be needed for the many attempts at making such a legacy a position of inferiority in the new land.

In that new country, social and political attitudes shaped and influenced the music. In the American south, the music that white musicians adapted while using African-derived instruments were ironically sharpened with a racist's point of view. It is beyond odd that the very instruments of the people they enslaved and oppressed gave them their soundtrack. One of my label's genre divisions at Music

World Entertainment is country, and I have seen how its rich history is sadly misunderstood and neglected.

The instrumental backbones of country and bluegrass music come from the banjo and guitar. For every country boy that ever plucked one or sang alongside it, there is a different origin story for where they came from. The true backstory to American string instruments, like those two and country music itself, is one that some southern music conservatives may need to learn.

There was mass criticism when Beyoncé and the Dixie Chicks performed for the televised "50th Country Music Awards" (CMA). Those who took the racial low roads, such as conservative country music purists, brought the argument that neither Beyoncé nor her genre could represent country music. Those in the know took to social media to point out how country music itself borrowed its roots from Black Americans. The list of famous Black country artists from DeFord Bailey and Charley Pride to Darius Rucker came up.

Black banjoist, Louis "Bebe" Vasnier, released numerous songs for the Louisiana Phonograph Company, including one of the earliest in 1891, "Brudder Rasmus" (sermons), which is barely audible but nonetheless preserved in the archives.

Still, even with such early proof of Black musicians in both country songwriting and instrumentation using the banjo, many diehards stuck to their stubborn beliefs that country was essentially, and always has been, a white American art form.

In the heat of the debate, the CMA was accused of their own whitewashing after they deleted all mentions of the performance from the organization's site and all social media. The CMA says it was because the footage was unapproved, yet they were still accused of giving in to those racist country conservatives after all. This highlights much of the nation's ignorance of not just country music and its beginnings but the influences behind all the most popular genres. If we start at the heart of that ignorance, we can trace the roots all the way back to slavery's beginnings.

First, let's ride on the sound of some fast-picking banjo and guitar to a Rockabilly vocalist who was rocking audiences way back in 1954. We'll go further later, but let's start there. One of Mississippi's native sons starts recording songs down south. The mix of country and R&B borrows heavily from African American vocal riffs and soul, while sung by a hip-swinging white boy, who flips into this new genre as hard as he does his hair.

Appropriation of the Black sound (or style) was not new in 1954, and Elvis Presley wouldn't be the first white artist to "taste" a little soul in his music, but he would be the biggest. "Blue Moon of Kentucky" was a Bill Monroe bluegrass song that Presley came in the business riding all the way to a throne. His later title of King of Rock and Roll was a well-disputed one in many communities—considering Chuck Berry, Little Richard, or even Fats Domino could have easily sported that crown in their eyes. Many musical genres try to pull in Presley's sound as their own, but his influences are clear if you listen.

Backing his sound were instruments that lend themselves so heavily to both rock and country that the myth behind them—being American-invented—is as ingrained as baseball and apple pie. Any American-born variation came from string instruments originating from much further away than Tupelo. The variety of gourd instruments that enslaved Africans used and crafted are both acknowledged and ignored in banjo lovers' circles, even exact origins remain hotly debated.

Regardless of where they came from, both the banjo and guitar were adopted and claimed by country music by the time the civil rights era kicked into full gear. To welcome in the times, Johnny Rebel, Louisiana's white supremacist songwriter, put out what was considered a hit in its day, "Move Them Niggers North."

All his songs frequently used that negative racial epithet as he echoed the white community's calls for segregation and praised the KKK (Ku Klux Klan). This was slightly controversial even in the '50s and '60s, and yet nearly every one of his titles uses the n-word liberally and sounds like Jim Crow party music. Parody or public opinion in that era?

Elvis Presley initially had his record label hiding his race, and with his sound alone he initially won over a new audience, from country to rock and its subgenres. With country music often tied to rural white southern people, it does music itself a disservice. Aside from overtly racist musicians like Johnny Rebel, numerous other country artists, while comparing their own upbringings in poverty, sympathized and called attention to the plight of Black America.

While blackface parodies had survived throughout the 1940s and '50s, up from minstrel shows through vaudeville on into TV with hugely watched shows like "Amos 'n' Andy," the country was waking up to offensive material. Also, the Black community used their collective voices to denounce racist imagery and music with the support of groups like the NAACP.

While the banjo and guitar helped racists strum up segregation, from the 1940s through the 1960s on, Black artists told the real story in their music. Among the best-selling folk albums of 1963 was Odetta Sings Folk Songs. By 1967, Aretha Franklin gave the Black community "Respect." Yet for every stride in a fight using music to express it, some other song rose to battle, with the conservatives using them as their own anthems to "anti" any Black cause.

For instance, the Freedom Riders were traveling the country getting up the Black vote. For them, country-western star Marty Robbins recorded "Ain't I Right," which sang out as a pro-segregation song, if any. Robbins's reference to one genre of music in his country hits like "Singing the Blues" and "Knee Deep in the Blues" takes us directly to a culture of people who brought that art form alive—the very ones being segregated.

    Yet by the 1970s, other chart-topping country artists show that not all their demographic was crooning for segregationists. In fact, between folk and country music, many of those artists became some of the most vocal musicians during the civil rights era.Meanwhile, those country music fans had a few legends among them who defied the all-white face of the genre. Charley Pride was an undisputed country music legend among whites and Blacks alike, with twenty-nine number one hit songs. The son of sharecroppers, born in 1930, he would be a voice for generations of country music lovers, even though his label hid his race until his music took hold. Once it did, he, like the 1920s-'30s–era harmonica-playing legend DeFord Bailey, could openly play at the Grand Ole Opry despite his color. In the 1930s, Bailey was practically king of the Opry as one of its most renowned acts to play the venue, along with other notables such as Uncle Dave Macon and Roy Acuff.

This shows that country music was not a byproduct of white American experience in its infancy. Black hillbilly string bands existed throughout the south, but the distinction came with the advent of vinyl recordings. When big money entered from those sales, the artists who were going to make the biggest profit off the phenomena were going to be white, first and foremost. By dividing "Black music" as blues, gospel, jazz, and eventually R&B/soul, from "white music," which would be country, bluegrass, and hillbilly, it gave white America claim to its own genres.

Like most segregated things in America, Blacks need not apply. The Darius Ruckers of today's commercial country music are not altogether rare, but there might be more if the genre didn't feel so exclusionary to Black musicians perhaps.

The conservative critics of Black participation in country music might watch the 2005 documentary on DeFord Bailey entitled "A Legend Lost in 2005" (Nashville Public Television/PBS). Inducted into the Country Music Hall of Fame in November of that same year, in 2007 Bailey was also given a Tribute Garden at the George Washington Carver Edible Park in Asheville. For a man who started out in the 1920s and brought acclaimed music to country lovers up through the 1940s, you would think his fame would be a solid reminder of Black artists' contributions to country music's early start.

Credited in the Encyclopedia of Country Music as "The most significant Black country star before World War II," Bailey should be a country music icon—for all the genre's fans. Men like Bailey and Pride were not rarities or oddities, they were descendants of pioneers of the sound. These musicians were reminders of the originators who were kept apart from their white contemporaries once money began being made. Yet it didn't seem to start that way, according to Bailey himself.

"One of the reasons country music was created by African Americans, as well as European Americans, is because Blacks and whites in rural communities in the south often worked and played together" — DeFord Bailey.

Sadly, since few Black string bands recorded or sold their music commercially during that era, and with many switching over to the blues to make more money where they were allowed, country music was left as an almost exclusively white music genre. Of the few who put their acts to wax were fiddler Howard Armstrong and the Tennessee Chocolate Drops trio. Rarely captured recordings of not just one but three double-sided 78 rpms recorded in 1930 for the Vocalion label leave but a few scattered copies in the world. The documentary Louie Bluie gives curious country music fans a more intimate look at this body of work.

There were many harmonica, fiddle, guitar, and banjo-playing groups to consider among those early artists. There were the Booker Orchestra quartet and the Mississippi Sheiks, the family group who recorded more than any of the others in their genre with upward of sixty or more tracks for a variety of labels in the 1930s. Their works were later covered by several artists, including one by Ray Charles.

This rich history debated whenever one Black performer dares to step into country music is exactly why a deeper education about the origins of modern American music must be explored. To marginalize "Black music" and make an area of it forbidden is just another white-only sign over a doorway.

In the 1950s, when those segregating signs hung over southern establishments, companies like Presley's label, Sun Records, and the man behind it, Sam Phillips, knew that the Black sound would sell—only with a white singer. By the time men like Charley Pride made it mainstream in country music and Chuck Berry was an icon in rock music, men like Phillips deftly took control of the sales. With a white breakout superstar like Elvis Presley, they could ride the soulful sound through TV, movies, and the top of the charts—all the way to the bank.

The nation's prejudice may not have allowed more than one or two Johnny Rebel musicians to popularize those ideas, but they still allowed him to exist, making dozens of derogatory songs over as many years. Such talk wasn't politically correct behavior in public even then, but nobody boycotted and stopped Rebel's recordings. And while they didn't want to see the Black sound, if presented by somebody like Elvis, white America would buy it into the millions.

The irony is there was no line between American Black and white music. One was born of the other and would not exist otherwise. The music lovers of today would still be ignorant of that had that whitewashing of the sound lasted.

The banjo's form and strumming that country musicians used was born first in African music, and many of the biggest country stars from bluegrass-playing Bill Monroe to honky-tonk favorite Hank Williams had their formative lessons taught at the knees of older Black artists. The act of call and response came from the need to create a feeling of community among Black people. The styles of vocal riffs were often born out of pain.

Many country music singers came from impoverished households themselves and felt they could adapt their stories to the hardscrabble existence these older Black artists sang about. In songs like "If That Ain't Country," David Allan Coe sings he's "workin' like a n**** for my room and board." While no fair parallel exists between slavery and rural southern white poverty, many country songs try to create just that.

No one could deny the healing benefits of the blues, and in its many forms it spread through even white musicians' songs. Nonetheless, any heart and soul behind them were lost in the money by the time commercial recording took over. For Black blues and country singers, like all money matters in America, the white majority ruled, and Blacks took longer to see any. This and other discriminatory practices inspired calls for freedom, reflected once again by the music—even from white musicians.

With the King of Rock crown on his head, even Presley couldn't escape the troubled times, and his own music had to eventually reflect them by 1968. With his "If

Can Dream," recorded after Martin Luther King, Jr.'s assassination, he used words from the speech in the song.

Songs like that and others showed American music had its racists and purists, but it also had artists who dared lend a supportive voice to the cause. They released songs that acknowledged the Black community as a part of its own. Later, country music staples like Brad Paisley would tell listeners that our forefathers would find pride in how the nation is trying to finally come together, and some of his songs brought progressive ideas to country music. His song "Accidental Racist" with rapper LL Cool J was a 2013 release that detailed the controversy surrounding the Confederate flag, both a sign of pride for southerners and a bold racist symbol.

Paisley also sings that as far as we've come, and as proud as our ancestors might be of that progress, there is still a tremendous road ahead. These collaborations show people of all colors coming together musically to effect a change.

Just as in the 1960s, when folk singers like Bob Dylan, Odetta, Joan Baez, Peter, Paul & Mary, Pete Seeger, Nina Simone, and Harry Belafonte joined the voices behind the civil rights movement, they brought with them the media and the public's attention.

Those banjo and guitar-plucking, folksy and soulful singers—white and Black—added a certain flavor to the early movement, all while those same instruments continued to back vicious parody songs that echoed slavery and Jim Crow's harshest intentions. Despite how used, positively or negatively, the controversial banjo is a great example of ignoring any influences from the slave community.

The music those African-inspired instruments make is profited off by those with intentions of controlling and repackaging it for the demographics that buy it. At one time, those were mostly white Americans who wanted something original to them, like baseball. Black men and women could not sell the music themselves and claim the throne like Elvis, yet their fingerprints remained all over it. Any bluegrass musician using a banjo to write a song demeaning Black people, or to defend their sole rights to the sound, is playing it in denial.

The biggest irony is that any of them holding that instrument would better understand the power and attraction of music if they traced it back to its birth, starting with the displacement and forced oppression of Africans and their culture. Once again, it was the raw experience that informed the sounds, the traditional tones that crafted the instruments, the handed-down techniques for playing them that invented the styling, and the conditions which innovated it.

If we follow the guitar and banjo through the debates and into the new global research around it, we find not just a testament to the endurance of the gourd instrument, but the people who accompanied it on its journey to America. Claims that the banjo or the guitar as we know them today did not originate from Africa, or that the style of singing and strumming were not influenced by it, are a part of the erasure of African American history. It is political, racial, and rightly controversial. The sound of a southern-plucked banjo points back to an era just before its appropriation as a white American innovation, when it strummed out the soundtrack of a terrible era for Black people. To remove the banjo's origins is to deny African artistry its rightful place at the nation's table.

The African Jola people, found throughout Guinea-Bissau, Gambia, and Senegal in West Africa, utilize an instrument called the akonting [AY-KON-TING], a lute-like object that, if you place alongside the modern banjo, you might think is a variation of the same. One African scholar thought so and took it on a journey.

Daniel Laemouahuma Jatta is well-spoken about the banjo's possible inspiration. As a skilled musician and scholar from the Gambia region of Africa, he spoke at the 2000 Banjo Collector's Conference and further opened the debate into just where that instrument originated. After he heard a bluegrass song on the radio, he immediately drew a parallel to his own native country's akonting. Part of the ongoing idea (which had been in place long before Jatta took the research to a new level) was that it had originated in West Africa as a gourd variety of instrument, then adapted into a purely American invention. White Western culture eventually erased any distinct line connecting its African roots.

It took thirty years for Jatta to trace that original line through intensive research. He found that the banjo was eerily like its African counterparts, in all their varied renderings. Yet most compelling for the argument of its

African roots is the technique for playing with a downstroking strum—exactly as Jatta's great-grandfather and other ancestors had done on the akonting in the Gambia and as he was taught by them. The designs are also undeniably similar, and yet banjo purists went so far as to accuse Jatta of claiming to invent the akonting himself.

Were the loud protestations against Jatta's research all about the research or more examples of appropriation and white Western superiority? The idea has always been that the banjo descended from lute-like instruments favored by West African griots [grē'ō], an inherited class of traveling musicians and poetic storytellers. Other instruments like the modern guitar or in Africa, the kora, were ones the griots crafted by hand and used.

However, instead of gourd resonators, like the banjo uses, those African griot style's resonators are wooden and not full-spike lutes like the banjo. The differences may seem minor, but to the communities of Africans and African descendants in America, details and origins are important to the preservation of not just Black history but of world facts. From its shape to the type of strum used upon it, the similarities are uncanny. It casts doubt on the banjo as a uniquely American instrument because its African influences are loud and apparent.

Instruments such as the kora were handed down from generation to generation, father to son. In this generation, Sona Joberteh, from the Gambia region in Africa, is the first female griot of her famous tribe. In addition to the kora, the Calabasas drum and other gourds as percussion tools are heavily used in their music, even today.

With these instruments as their backbeat, it was the job of a griot to perform the original tribal teachings orally.

Music was the bedding for these keepers of African history. As royal advisers in African societies, they were born into their duties and not appointed. That role as music historian could flourish through songs, spoken word, poetry, dance, and instrumental expression, all to express stories of their ancestry.

Of the number of noted West African lute varieties, those individuals who dared contradict Jatta's claim that the akonting is an ancestor of these instruments his griot ancestors used ask where it has been hiding in history. They claim it wouldn't have escaped cataloging by Western scholars. Therefore, to them, the akonting was a fabrication just because it didn't find its way into the books of early researchers listing all the continent's loot. With undoubtedly missing pieces to the musical puzzle, the banjo's controversy opens a door to questions about all the rest of our musical heritage. What are the true origins of what we all now call

American music? Is all this fuss because of its apparent power?

Daniel Laemouahuma Jatta proved the playing styles and even the songs and cadences that go with the akonting/banjo were music that his Gambian people in Africa had played for many generations. In taking a simple bluegrass country sound and picking out the distinct sounds of an ancient instrument from his homeland, he also picked the lock on a door that had long closed on historical facts. The guitar, the banjo, the plucking styles, the songs—all point back in one direction: Africa.

"Slaves are usually expected to sing as well as to work. A silent slave is not liked by masters or overseers.... This may account for the almost constant singing heard in the southern states. I have often been utterly astonished, since I came north, to find persons who spoke of the singing among slaves as evidence of their contentment and happiness. It is impossible to conceive of a greater mistake.

Slaves sing most when they are most unhappy. The songs of the slaves represent the sorrows of his life; and he is relieved by them only as an aching heart is relieved by its tears. At least such is my experience."

—*Frederick Douglass*

CHAPTER THREE

MESSAGE IN THE MUSIC

While the notion that Africans were inferior or savage may have helped support the practice of slavery, there was no indication they were not initially respected for their governing abilities and intelligence prior to enslavement. That didn't stop the fear and even envy of their strength by the slaveholding community. Once in America, there was a growing racial disparity between Africans and whites that led to abusive discrimination based on ideas of white supremacy.

The hatred that grew from such ignorance led to horrors the African people had never experienced. While slavery has existed in many forms all over the planet, in Africa the system was not so brutal, nor did it involve the elements of hate based on race or tribe. If it had been just about owning a commodity, and slaves themselves were valued as human beings, would the atrocities that took place over hundreds of years have existed? Even cattle were treated better, as commodities go. The mean-tempered treatments, family separations, molestations, rapes, murders, and lynchings all carried an extra added element of hate and sadistic superiority.

Having to work under such conditions made the yoke of slavery something not just seemingly inescapable but, as told by the Christian doctrines that helped enslave them, a punishment by God. A curse upon their race from the biblical figure Noah upon the descendants of Ham was adopted by enslavers who deemed it the African's fate.

With no means of liberation, homesick, and abused in a land unfamiliar to them, how hard was it to sing that first note? It makes us examine the effects and benefits of music as a form of therapy and release. There arose misconception by slave owners that these songs and ring dances were signs of contentment from people who were happy with their conditions. Why would they dance and sing so if they were not celebrating life? They never assumed that these were methods for coping with the horror as well.

The white men needed labor, and Africans were there to provide it. There was nothing joyous about the arrangement. The enslavers' use of Native Americans as slaves proved unsuccessful, as many succumbed to disease and died. Suicide was not uncommon either. As far as rebellions go, they had warrior tribes to help defend their freedom from the region itself many times. They would crash the colonizers' sadistic party by just raiding it. With unity of tribes, braves had numbers and weapons that imported Africans, torn from their tribes, did not. They were captives with few intact family ties, no knowledge of the landscapes, and, therefore, were less likely to have the power behind a revolt or the means for a mass escape. They were experienced farmers when it came to crops and livestock and offered, even shipped from as far as the African coast, cheap labor for the colonizers who were not about to let them walk free. The enslavers tolerated the culture and the multi-flavored "slave music" that came with it because the food was tasty, they had before been choking on old Puritan hymns, and the free labor naturally proved to be useful to them.

Music also served other functions in the captives' daily lives, such as to celebrate and commemorate important events like births, deaths, or weddings. Importantly, songs were an oral history tool with reading and writing prohibited for them. What they had, and often even memorized in place of writing or even reading it, was the recitation of the Christian Bible.

Its scriptures and texts became symbolic means of escape and communication and played one of the most important roles in both their music and their efforts to gain freedom. A question I ask my students is, "Since the Black church is so significant to modern music, where did it start?

Because if religion among slaves was at first forbidden, who finally decided to appoint the preachers?"

Before we get into that history, let me note that the Black church and its music are like a cup of water to Black communities: one part holds, while the other part quenches them. To find a church service without a soul-stirring choir or at least a hymn-heavy organist is altogether rare. Voices in unison in a church would be comprised of the entire community, groups young and old, mostly family members.

No matter how we find that the church came about for African descendants, it was upheld because of its ability to keep together families. That bond of love and the need to preserve it stands behind how African captives and their offspring learned to survive. Strength in numbers and a motivation for a better life for everyone.

It's important to the foundations of the songs we sing and the way art, culture, and traditions are used in every household, to understand the role family and community had in creating, sharing, and passing down music and culture.

Family came together in the safest way in the Black church. It brought everyone away from their toils and labor, worries and fears, into a place where everyone could be accounted for and have a sense of a tribe (something the African people thrived on in their homeland). To leave that was not easy. Often, especially in the American south, the tearing apart of a family once it was formed was a common and cruel practice.

Having forged that unity, it would have been a devastation to have it taken away. In places where plantation owners favored keeping families together, those Sunday gatherings (passed down to this day) were a welcomed event. Food, fun, and loving time to bond marked those occasions to enjoy the time out of oppression. To voluntarily leave your family took a lot more than one might imagine.

Once formed, those bonds are nearly unbreakable. Even in the absence of a loved one, the longing for them remains. So, to the recent debates over what a slave would or wouldn't do to free themselves, one considers the weight of rebellion and what it does to family. Think of the loneliness behind deserting them while freeing yourself. The certainty of death or punishment at the hands of any uprising or escape.

To better help us, we should walk a mile in their shoes. Let's put us there.

Pick any year before 1865 in America and jump in as a man or woman enslaved by a white slave master. You have a few choices: save any money you're lucky to make or inherit and attempt to buy you and your family free. Or run. To do so, you all must agree to go together, from the crying and still nursing babies to the old and from years of hard labor. You need to run at least 90 miles in some cases, north or to wherever Black folks aren't held in chains by law

Ready. Set. Go!

Not so fast…

Once off the plantation, should you all be so lucky to have escaped it or bought your way free, a new set of challenges await. Namely, feeding everyone and staying alive. Even free, to keep from returning to bondage you must avoid being arrested for infractions considered taboo for Black people, even up north. Loitering, loud laughter, wild behavior, or just extreme poverty could make you look unfit or immoral to the police who, like now, were ready to answer the call for your removal.

If you were free and Black in the south, that freedom hung by a precarious thread. Tight laws that included scrutiny on behavior and profiling of free Black people were convenient snares to rope them back into slavery. These Expulsion Laws kept a threat hanging over the very idea of a free Black person, who had to follow impossible expectations to maintain that freedom. You had a limited time to secure housing, employment, or trade, or you were outside of the law. If still saving to free other family members, you must work double-time.

Had you broken the slightest rule while free, you would have had to beg for leniency in court if you landed there, with everything you worked so hard to get to on the line. Years might pass before enough money got saved for any of this, and very few would risk losing their family forever. If you knew leaving them would lead to all of this and possibly a continued separation, might you have weighed freedom and its hopes against what you stood to lose?

Look at the few cases in legal history of enslaved families even petitioning to be reunited, such as with freeborn men and women asking to be put into slavery to join family. Or when a free woman named Percy Ann Martin, in North Carolina, asked the judge to "reduce her to slavery" as "she was attached to her husband and does not wish to be separated from him." Another man in Virginia declared the same, saying he "would prefer returning to slavery to losing the society of his wife."

Don't think this wasn't exploited. How heinous for them to enslave the body and play on the heart. Pro-slavery talkers proclaimed it proof free Blacks could not maintain their status due to their unfitness. Nothing said about family or feelings and commitments. Poorer slaveholders enjoyed the cheaper labor of a formerly freed Black person returning to the unpaid labor pool. Some buyers had only to pay a fraction of the court fees on top of the sale, and it afforded even those with meager finances to have a slave.

These decisions to return to bondage perplexed the hardworking abolitionists, who also failed to recognize the power of the family bond, apparently. This was not about love of the master and the conditions of his household, rather, attachments to any substantial community the people forged during years of service there. The Black community had been forged in a communal bond that made individualism dangerous during slavery. Where is freedom in isolation, with no one you love to share it with?

During slavery, the idea that something would happen to your wife, daughter, husband, or son while they remain enslaved and you are free would be a heavy one, when considering whose keep they are in. The slaveholders and their foremen that made slavery the hell it was had no problem hurting, maiming, killing, or selling off a family member to parts unknown overnight. It's easy to control someone when the life of their ninety-year-old elder or their nine-day-old son is on the line, and slaveholders did just that as a threat against escape and a deterrent to individualized freedom.

What kept the conditions manageable was the community-stabilizing institution of the church. In any denomination, it filled the pews with large groups of families and friends, and their music closed the circle. In those antebellum slave quarters, instrumentalists held a prestigious advantage as their status revived social time. Only the reverends and "musicianers" enjoyed such a status.

The church itself was an event, but that day off provided time for further gathering. In a social event called The Frolic, the people got to come together in ways besides prayer meetings on Sunday. While not yet the political or rebellious force they would become in some areas, these gatherings initially held the community together with the impact of music, which remained a common element among them no matter the changing times.

Emancipation, and later Reconstruction, affected the people in its degree of rapid change, yet the secular ministers and musicians would still play a major role in Black social and cultural life. Their music brought them all together to rejuvenate burdened spirits in ways Sunday meetings did not. These secular slave quarter events shaped the reverence held for instrumentalists, vocalists, and spiritual singers of that time.

But how did they get there, out of the African Muslims, Yoruban, and such distinct tribesmen gathered from the continent? How did the preacher, who is the quintessential bandleader of a feel-good service in the Black church, become such a force?

Divided along social and economic lines as well as interpretations and practices, the Black church is widespread in its forms. It is not one roof housing all people; the term simply names all those descended from African captives once they formed a community of faith. From a 1758 registry, some notes about the earliest Black churches in America can be traced. Prior to Christianity taking hold on the plantations, early colonizing slaveholders saw a serious threat in the congregation and communication between their slaves.

In one historical account, a slave stated, "The white folks would come in when the colored people would have prayer meeting and whip every one of them. Most of them thought that when colored people were praying it was against them."

When they could gather to worship, they were closely monitored. The African captives would initially be allowed to attend the slaveholders' local services, seated in the rear or just outside the doors, and only permitted to leave when raising a finger, so the foreman could count who was where (a practice that continued in my own youth attending church in Alabama in the 1960s).

In early services, they had to demonstrate obedience, and it was well-emphasized with plenty of references to their role in bondage as dictated in parts of the Bible, as in, "Slaves, obey your masters." Once that lesson was firmly entrenched, memorized, and repeated, what was the harm in letting one of them, the most able to convey the core messages as taught, to lead a small service themselves for their own people?

In his book The Negro Church in America, E. Franklin Frazier notes, "Methodist and Baptist denominations were separate church organizations based upon distinctions of color and what were considered standards of civilized behavior." That sort of so-called civilized approach to worship might have gotten an approving nod from the white community over time, leading to the formations of those churches in the first place.

Sometime around 1758, before the American Revolution, the African Baptist or "Bluestone" Church began services on William Byrd's plantation in Virginia. The African worshippers adopted their beliefs in distinct ways such as total immersion adult-only baptism. The First Colored Church (later to become the First African Baptist Church of Savannah, Georgia) followed in 1777 as the oldest Black church in North America. Communication between the organizations occurred as they grew.

By 1787 in Philadelphia, the Free African Society elected Richard Allen and Absalom Jones to spread the orders nationally until they eventually built a church on July 17, 1794. By the time of emancipation, the church as a collective was well-established as its own institution.

Once launched, the churches became places of safety and refuge, especially post–Civil War. In 1867, shortly after emancipation, thirty-eight Black parishioners of the mostly white Fairfield Baptist Church in Virginia petitioned to "place ourselves where we could best promote our mutual good ... and a separate church organization as the best possible way." They were granted that in a unanimously decided vote, leading to the Shiloh Baptist Church.

With the widespread nature of the services, it is no wonder so many diverse practices formed, some still managing to subtly blend in aspects of traditional African ritual as well as the new practices developed. The devotional, or opening prayer, was often itself musical and usually kicked off by someone as the lead with others blending in. It was a summation of the hard lives they led by calling for mercy until rapid praise would whip them into shape to face more. A call and response with "Amen!" "Hallelujah!" and "Show me favor!" echoed around the singing. Hymns, or a choir marching in singing one, often followed, with many parishioners' voices joining in. The sermon would be the meat to the meeting and a style of serving itself with echoes of call and response, or melodious forms of speaking from the preacher. A dramatic, poetic, deeply emotional delivery is what he was expected to bring. Whether flamboyantly or not, delivering the message is what his role was.

Churches grew; by 1886 they formed the National Baptist Convention, as one example, and cemented the position of Black-controlled worship solely to the people themselves, reducing white ministers' involvements altogether. Remnants of their songs and hymns, lessons and practices would remain, one of which is ironically tied to the transatlantic slave trade and a musical staple in the Black church.

"Amazing Grace," one of the world's most popular hymns and best known as a staple in the Black church, was penned by John Newton, a former slave trader. The son of a Puritan mother, Newton was born in 1725 in London and raised at sea by his strict father after her death. He joined the British Navy later in life, and after a demotion ended up with the rank of common seaman. Continuing to sail, he later commandeered a slave ship. After abandonment in West Africa by his crew, he ended up stranded there and eventually was caught up in his own adventures with an African princess. However, it was on his trip home that the ship met with a storm that threatened to sink it. It was during his fervent prayers for God's intervention that the ship found a miracle while in the middle of sinking.

Cargo that moved during tossing of the ship filled the breach and stopped the water from flowing onboard until they reached safe shores. Newton saw this as a divine intervention, and it became his motivation for conversion to a new faith. As a Christian, he gradually embraced reform and started to see African captives in a more compassionate light. Even so, as captain of two different slave ships, he continued selling and transporting Africans on at least three added voyages.

After his retirement, he was still actively investing in the trade, even as he entered the order as an Anglican priest and went on to write 280 hymns, including "Amazing Grace," published in Olney Hymns in 1779. It took a full thirty-plus years for him to renounce the slave trade and back it by publishing a pamphlet titled, "Thoughts Upon the Slave Trade," which offered detailed accounts of the trauma and conditions captives faced.

He eventually even apologized and sent his pamphlet to every member of Parliament. It also was widely printed throughout the region. Once slavery was outlawed in Great

Britain in 1807, Newton was still alive to see it. A movie, Amazing Grace, and a Broadway show about his life detail the events (although often more colorfully than the actual ones) of his inevitable influence on the passage of the Slave Trade Act and of that legendary song.

Any songs gifted to slaves (always able to see multiple uses for any one thing) were used in that way. How influential were escapees' spiritual songs in helping fugitives flee slavery and then survive it once the codes became creeds? Very, according to history. Hidden down in a song, we find encouragement for both bravery and ingenuity in escaping servitude.

Those spirituals are only one example of how a song became a key to free first their inner slave from the emotional and spiritual battle against depression, fatigue, and traumatic stress. I wonder: how could anyone run anywhere with the baggage of that mental burden on their backs? And, of course, actual chains.

The antebellum period in America—pre-Civil War and post-War of 1812—kicked off with the north's sudden economic growth due to the Industrial Revolution and in the south from the cotton gin. Caught in the middle, and a hot-button issue for abolitionists, was the African community. Even though the institution of slavery wasn't popular with many Americans, it was so ingrained into society, few felt anything could be done about it except for the abolitionist community, chief among them Quakers and Puritans.

With slavery being the basis of an entire region's economy—particularly the south—it stayed entrenched as a system for over four centuries. To avoid chaos and the dismantling of the union between the north and the south, abolishing slavery was stalled for as long as possible among the founding fathers. No one was looking for that level of trouble. Eventually, the south did secede from the union and, in 1861, the country entered the Civil War.

While the antebellum period was taking place, and the Underground Railroad system set up by the abolitionists began to stir, word of the Haitian revolution in the background inspired the African American community to want to fight their conditions as well. Those who could not fight their battles in court and sue for it bought their freedom after years of saving their labor wages, and they escaped with their lives that way. This led to a larger number of freedmen and women who founded communities of their own in cities that accommodated them. Still, the pressure in those places to fit in was great.

In Canada, escaped slaves had to work to acquire land that was to be kept at a certain caliber to be accepted into the community at-large. Some purchased land as far as Buxton (and originally the Elgin Settlement) in Ontario, Canada, where the Underground Railroad made its northernmost stop for escaped slaves. On behalf of post-emancipation checkups on former slaves, a Freedmen's Inquiry Commission, run by the Secretary of War, went up there to collect information on their status. War secretary Dr. Samuel Gridley Howe took a reporter along with him in 1863 and had this to say about the Canadian province of Buxton:

"Buxton is certainly a very interesting place. Sixteen years ago, it was a wilderness.... Twenty years ago most of them [inhabitants] were slaves, who owned nothing, not even their children. Now they own themselves; they own their houses and farms; they have their wives and children about them. They are the enfranchised citizens of a government that protects their rights.... The present condition of all these colonists as compared with their former one is remarkable.... This settlement is a perfect success ..."

What pressure was there in those communities to be the perfect version of a freed slave, and how did they cope? An excellent read on this is found in Stamped from the Beginning: The Definitive History of Racist Ideas in America by Ibram X. Kendi. This gives us a look at how certain abolitionists' "rules of engagement" encouraged an impossible position for the enslaved. They gave advice on everything from keeping from bad habits and vices (i.e., drinking, smoking, or cursing) to getting and staying married, going to church, abstaining from being too loud, never being disorderly, and learning the basics of reading and writing.

The ways of old might have included their desires to gather in ring shouts, patting juba, or other exciting forms of expression. Now, quiet hymns were advised instead. No Holy Ghost shouting in these prim conditions; no loud calling and responding either. It was another way of suppressing their traditional customs and instincts, although the advisers—the abolitionists—were well-intentioned.

To behave this way, they taught, would help foster respectability for Black people in the eyes of racists. It would overturn old ideas that white was the only right when it came to superiority and respectability. Kendi writes that this was in effect "uplift suasion," a tool for convincing white racists to abandon their notions and accept a gentrified version of the Black people they hated.

This was an impossible if not ridiculous notion—that Black people had to be picture perfect in their eyes to live in peace, especially when those hating them carried out all those forbidden behaviors daily. A plantation owner could get drunk and disorderly enough to beat his slave to death and then rape his slave's wife when done. In court, his drunkenness would be taken into consideration, along with his position in society, and he would be then fined or gently admonished and sent back home to rinse and repeat.

A Black man or woman so much as skipping church or skipping to church on Sunday, laughing too loud, dancing too vulgarly, or drinking too much was a disgrace—a shameful representation, not just of himself and his family but to his entire race. As Kendi states, "The burden of race relations was placed squarely on the shoulders of Black Americans."

Imagine this: That is the weight that had to be carried daily. It's no wonder older generations kept such strict rules about how we looked, dressed, behaved, and spoke "in front of white folks" so as not to appear as inferior in their minds. The finest dressed, most articulate and refined Black man of that era would have still been a candidate for a hard lynching if he offended.

One of my older relatives used to insist on there once being laughing barrels. It sounded so preposterous, I dismissed it for most of my life, but that didn't erase it as a fact. On a plantation, anyone enslaved there who was too jolly and wanted to smile or shout because of it found that desire as suppressed as a drumbeat. If too boisterous, he or she had to stick their heads down in and stifle the impulse in that "laughing barrel." It's a wonder smiles could even be passed down to us, coming from such oppressive conditions.

It was not that abolitionists meant to demean those they were trying to help free with advice to "tone it down a little." There was no doubt they thought these tactics would empower the people and produce genuine respect from whites.

Nice work if you can get it. Those that did, dug in. But what happened if you didn't "fit in" by keeping to these rules as a newly free person? Whether during slavery or just after the emancipation period, the lives of anyone, fresh off a plantation or born on one, were always hanging in the balance between freedom and being some man's property.

Even Black people who had never been a slave faced the threat of becoming one through the prison industrial complex, which was as ominous then as it is now. In what was called a convict-leasing system, any of those unfortunate individuals who ended up in a court of law, particularly in the south, could end up prisoners. And that was just another word for slave, as they were "sold" by states, such as my adopted home, Texas, and "lent" to privately owned outfits that usually ended up being a plantation of some kind—meaning a master, a foreman, and a whole heap of forced backbreaking work.

If you were where there were sugar plantations as a prisoner (or slave), you hoisted cane. If near the mines, you hauled coal. If near industry, you hefted steel; if next to cotton, you damn sure had to pick some. Such labor built the Texas Capitol building from the ground up. It became a business that was as popular as it was profitable.

The Imperial Sugar Co. built up around the abuse taking place of imprisoned workers, who were getting the lash as frequently and as sadistically as those who had been on a pre-emancipation southern plantation. Just as they had in those fields, the workers used music and chants to not only keep time and pace to the workload but to unite in voice and uplift in spirit. Many of these songs, such as the ones created by the railroad tie-tampers (which we also cover here), depict back-cracking work, often under a hellishly hot sun and an even hotter whip.

Did the state care about such beatings and neglect? Not if there was no money being lost (or further gained) by the leased-out labor. Any sick individual could carry out abuse on these men and sometimes women because there was no specific regulation that said they couldn't.

When almost 4,000 prisoners can die under such conditions in a state like Texas alone, you can imagine what Georgia, Alabama, Virginia, and other states' tallies looked like. If one of them died, they'd go get more. From the mid-1800s on into late Reconstruction, this proliferated, and many lives were lost.

Only the pain in the music remains to tell us what those people endured. When they uncovered a burial ground of these former prisoners whose bodies showed the wear and disease and defeat of slavery their whole lives, the truth resurfaced. Now, in 2018, everyone can see the proof of the horror show a corrupt legal system perpetrated for years. Can anyone look at the prison system today, count the young Black men held there, and not see the pattern even today?

Anyone who made it out on the Underground Railroad, or by other means of escape such as saving and buying their freedom, ultimately gathered and at least proved they could get along as a self-contained community—off the plantation. The churches and trades in those places started to grow from their own businesses and fraternal orders. These moves bonded the ties between them and helped to eventually build them safer and more productive havens—like the infamous but ill-fated Black Wall Street.

This community in the Greenwood section of Tulsa, Oklahoma, became one of those successful concentrations of upwardly mobile African American businesses until the Tulsa race riot of 1921, when racial envy and hatred once again tore the people away from all they'd built. On their own as freemen, they could freely make money, love, or music all day long; on the plantations in Georgia, there was a law in place that decreed, "Whatever master or overseer shall permit his slaves to beat, blow horns or loud instruments 'shall forfeit thirty shillings sterling for every such offense.'" Some slaveholding music hater was steadily trying to kill the vibe.

The only way to peace seemed to be conforming or at least adapting what was handed to them, including the meaning and intent behind the dry hymns, and giving them life. Using the simplest tool—the human voice—they could find a way.

The term "spiritual" first derived from the King James Bible translation of Ephesians 5:19: "Speaking to yourselves in psalms and hymns and spiritual songs, singing and making melody in your heart to the Lord." It is historically one of the largest and most important forms of American folksong. It formed as that distinct sound due to the call and response form, with a leader improvising a line of text and a chorus of singers providing a solid refrain in unison.

Because the vocal style ran in a freestyle nature, it was very challenging for early publishers of spirituals to document them accurately. There are also different forms of them, with the most popular called the "sorrow songs," which were intense, slow, and melancholic. Examples include "Sometimes I Feel like a Motherless Child" and "Nobody Knows the Trouble I've Seen." Both songs describe their empathy with the suffering Christ.

Other forms of spirituals were more pleasant. Known as "jubilees" or "camp meeting songs," they were fast and more rhythmic. Examples include "Rock my Soul in the Bosom of Abraham" and "Fare Ye Well."

The coded songs could fully express their frustration and anguish over the tasks and their conditions. In them, they could reminisce of better places and times while dreaming of a life somewhere else someday. Using short phrases of around two to three bars, in synchronized chants and beats using hands or tools, music could save the day in ways that hid their meanings. For example, songs like "Ole Pharaoh" disguises evil slaveowners as rascally animals. They could complain right in the open, even with a mean foreman clapping along, because it made them work hard and fast.

Believing these were happy laborers, slaveholders missed the comparison of Egyptian slavery to their own. With music regulating the pace, the captives could keep up their expected quotas and work quickly, thus avoiding a lashing or two. It no doubt made the monotony and tediously repetitive nature of the work easier to handle, and the watching slaveholders stayed blissfully unaware of any underpinning messages in the music.

Songs like "Almost Over" and "Archangel Open the Door," later published in 1867 as "Slave Songs of the United States" by Applewood Books, depict in their titles alone the people begging for divine help in escaping their woes and for spiritual relief. However, it wasn't always the music of misery seeking God's helping hand; the worldwide phenomenon known as "carnival," expressed in a variety of ways from Brazil to England, is a perfect expression of the slave resistance in how their culture persisted in the most colorful of rebellions.

Modern dance, such as Brazilian martial arts (Capoeira: "Cap-ee-or-rah") and even later forms such as breakdancing, came from those ancestral moves. Even with the widespread nature of the slave trade, it's not a coincidence how many dances or melodies, called by different names depending on the region, are similar.

An eyewitness described how in the 1850s he saw dancing in New Orleans. Here the account sounds very much like modern breakdancing circles:

"The bamboula still roars and rattles, twangs, contorts, and tumbles in terrible earnest while we stand and talk ... the music changes. The rhythm stretches out heathenish and ragged. The quick contagion is caught by a few in the crowd, who take it up with spirited smitings of the bare sole upon the ground and of open hands upon the thighs. From a spot near the musicians a single male voice, heavy and sonorous, rises in improvisation—the Mandingoes brought that art from Africa—and in a moment many others have joined in the refrain, male voices in rolling, bellowing

resonance, female responding in high piercing unison." — George Washington Cable. From Legacies of Slavery: Dance by Dr. Alan Rice.

The plantation dance, or ring shouting, which was also widespread, is another example of how the sense of community built upon both the music and the dances. Out of these communal African moves that spread through the southern plantations and as far as the Caribbean came the juba or hambone in the US (hambonin), in a movement which took place in groups centered around two dancers.

Pattin' juba would look like a series of pats, slaps, stomps, and smacks of various parts of the body from the face and cheeks to the arms and chest. This body-beatboxing of sorts would keep time for the dancers in a formation called the walkaround. These dances were commonplace in these settings on each continent, where the transported African community was given a chance to come together.

Ring shouts were their only means to unite both voice and presence in a way that was also invigorating after the labors of the plantation workday. It gave them a chance to unbox their voices and emotions in the same way some tribes "ululate" in ritual or religious cries, and the experience would move their bodies into celebration, clapping, stomping, and leaping to the rhythms. Not unlike a form of prayer and jubilation were dances behind the music. Moving counterclockwise, the call and response chanting went back and forth, with the percussive undertones of sticks or boots beating or stomping up a rhythm. This was a message of unity in motion.

As the Christian influence among them grew, those enslaved who adopted its customs and beliefs found restrictions in what they could and could not do—like it being unholy to cross the feet while dancing. Imagine how that restricted even their dance moves! After Sunday service, when the heavy preaching was done, barns were converted into praise houses with the sounds of a ring shout in progress. The enslaved would be overcome with the spirit, seemingly possessed of it in their passionate expressions; it was something slaveholders rightly feared for its power. Yet anyone trying to stop them found themselves powerless as the phenomena grew.

Sometime around the Civil War, people who came in from southern coastal areas such as the Georgia Islands started documenting these sessions—particularly in South Carolina and Louisiana, where it persisted into the twentieth century. As long as the slave trade continued, new groups of Africans would appear regularly and, thus, the bridge between the enslaved Africans and their people and homeland remained open. The music, art, food, and dance could continue to spread anew, despite the efforts of the slaveholders to suppress it.

It took more than the force of the people's will to be free to get them there. It took supporters from the white community to create channels to areas where they could be. Meanwhile, the country was grappling with slavery and debating its continued enforcement. The controversial Revolutionary War is what led to northern states abolishing slavery. After the American Revolution (1775-'83), northern colonists began to link the oppression of African slaves to their own oppression by the British and to call for slavery's abolition.

This gave a place for potential freedom in the minds of both abolitionists and captives, and getting "up north," where these ideas were practiced, was a goal. In lieu of returning to their true homeland, any form of freedom from the plantations would do. The colony of Pennsylvania was established in 1681 when King Charles II gave William Penn, an English Quaker, a large land grant in America to pay off a debt owed to his family. William Penn had been jailed numerous times for his beliefs. Quakers are known as the Religious Society of Friends, founded in England in the seventeenth century by George Fox. However, after persecution for his beliefs, William Penn went on to found Pennsylvania as a haven for religious freedom and tolerance. After a few years, several thousand of his friends began to move there from Britain.

The Quakers took up the cause of protecting Native American rights initially. They formed the earliest abolitionists. In 1758, Quakers in Philadelphia were ordered to stop buying and selling slaves; by the 1780s, all Quakers had abolished owning any. The Quakers were also the first organized group to actively help them escape. George Washington was said to have complained of Quakers attempting to help one of his slaves get free.

In the early 1800s, Quaker abolitionist Isaac T. Hopper set up a network in Philadelphia that helped slaves on the run. At the same time, Quakers in North Carolina established abolitionist groups that laid the groundwork for routes and shelters for escapees. Thereafter, the African

Methodist Episcopal Church, established in 1816, was another proactive religious group helping fugitive slaves.

Quakers of the eighteenth and nineteenth centuries were very aware that their order had once held slaves—people who had worked but had not been paid. Beyond paying for sins of the Society of Friends by ending slavery, they looked to the education of the freed people.

It was a Quaker and former slaveowner, Richard Humphries, who left a similar bequest which laid the foundations for what is now Cheyney University, the oldest historically Black school. Above the oppressive weight of slavery in the south and in regions where abolitionists protected their right to life, both education and freedom waited. The word about being away from the yoke of slave masters spread, and several brave souls dared to seek freedom for themselves. Besides the abolitionists, it was the early Black church that provided avenues for escape.

Despite the evangelicalism that grew out of America's Second Great Awakening, Black Americans soon realized the hypocrisy and weaknesses of their fellow congregation members and decided as a group to divest. Led by Richard Allen (1760-1831) since 1787, members in Philadelphia started their own organization with the African Methodist Episcopal (AME) Church by 1815. Baptists in the Black community increased significantly also over the years.

By 1846, the AME Church had swelled to 17,375 members. The Black community took to the new denominations and autonomy from the white church and dug in to form what is now the backbone of most of its citizens. Meanwhile, in the south, slavery was still white slaveholders' main faith, and the problem of their "property" getting a mind of their own, even about serving God, would always be one needing to be controlled.

This led me to question why any southern white plantation owner would hand the keys to spiritual and emotional freedom to his slaves, especially given how the faith was eventually used for physical escapes as well.

I've read in the research that itinerant preachers brought sermons and spirituals that helped them pass from plantation to plantation. Still, how many preachers could roam from farm to estate carrying mysterious codes, whether slaveholders knew the meaning or not? Did a traveling preacher show up at Marse John's house, get to have a bush meeting or camp meet with a gathering of his slaves, and leave them with the understanding of what it all meant?

It seems a stretch, but when you pull back the documents and biographies of those who lived to share their stories, you can piece together how it could happen. Yet those few can't represent the whole, and one must assume the preaching those early plantation workers got was homegrown and foreman-supervised, at least initially. The "corn ditties," as they called them, were not always opportunities for slaves to get bulletins on escape plans. Most gatherings no doubt did what they intended—got everyone away from work in a community of worship and praise.

The 1850 Protestant City-Revival Movement led to innovation of the music, as large-scale revival meetings became more popular, and the songs morphed again to accommodate the grand mix of folks singing them.

The sorrow songs of the Negro spiritual, with sadder, more lamenting lyrics, weren't as motivating for the growing crowds. They wanted hope, and the parts of the Bible that promised it were adapted into songs every attendant could aspire to.

Being "saved" was akin to being free for those work-weary folks, and if they couldn't get it bodily, the spirit would do—for now. "Sweet Canaan, the Promised Land," were real places, the music told them, and in time, with mercy, they would get there. It made sense for those brave enough to scheme a way off those plantations to cleverly adapt the words to fit their escape plans. If nothing else, work songs allowed them to complain out in the open and never get called on it because, after all, it was just an old song.

Documented in 1839 by a Washington newspaper, Jim, an escaped slave, was caught and tortured for his plan to go north following an "underground railroad to Boston." Vigilance committees began to form to protect escaped slaves from bounty hunters. The ingenuity of using music for coding became a method of communication between slaves, such as made famous by Harriet Tubman. Tubman is the most well-known of all "conductors" of the Underground Railroad, which became the most famous conduit to freedom. She successfully relayed messages to fugitive slaves through songs to avoid translation by slave owners and bounty hunters. Many fugitives headed for Canada due to the Fugitive Slave Acts, and she helped in that escape route as well.

The first Exclusion Laws, passed around 1793, allowed local governments to apprehend and extradite escaped slaves from within the borders of free states back to their point of origin and to punish anyone helping fugitives. Some northern states tried to combat this with Personal Liberty Laws, which were struck down by the Supreme Court in 1842.

The Fugitive Slave Act of 1850 was designed to strengthen the previous law, which was felt by southern states to be inadequately enforced. This update created harsher penalties and set up a system of commissioners that promoted favoritism toward slave owners and led to some freed slaves' recapturing. For an escaped slave, northern states were a risk, but for courageous people like Harriet, it was one worth taking.

What was an Underground Railroad? It was a passage to freedom—the best way an escapee could muster, using whatever help they could raise. It started out as an abolitionists' group sneaking and freeing a slave or two or passing the message to workers who used their help later to run away.

It was a railway in that at each stage along the way, some help would have been found. The first stage would have to have been awareness of it. How did people know where to go and whom to trust? How did they know a certain word meant one thing to white folks and another to the white people who were helping them escape?

I wonder if that first abolitionist/slave conversation went something like this:

"Sarah, if you want to get away from the Jones plantation, I have a safe way. You can trust me and my friends to help you. Meet me down by the old red barn south of the plantation at sundown and be ready to run!"

Did Sarah trust them? Somebody must have, because it became a means for hundreds of slaves to escape over many years. Other times, a captive would hear from someone else if he was loaned out to work on another farm about a way to freedom, and he'd pass it on. They might have agreed to terms and words beforehand that would signify ready points, allies, and cautionary warnings.

Once the people along each stage established their support systems, an escapee could make it to the old red barn to meet someone who would hide them in a wagon until they got to a safe house miles away. There they would be hidden in secret rooms and crawl spaces until the coast was clear for the next stage. Once over state lines where slavery was outlawed, another set of supporters, Freedmen, or more abolitionists and their friends would help the escapee find housing, employment, and make plans for freeing their families.

But they had to get there first. That call outside the window as the sun went down that asked them to "steal away" was more than Old Ben singing. Old Ben had heard the word, and his message was down in it if you were in the know. Somebody would have told you in a church gathering or in the field about what those words would mean and how to use signposts to get away. Because they used the language that conductors used, "agents" were the ones trusted to carry messages and codes and intercede should anyone be caught.

According to the Harriet Tubman Historical Society, some keywords they used as codes emerged over time and were recorded after slavery, including:

Agent/Coordinator: Plotted escape and made contacts

Canaan: Canada

Conductor: Person who directly transported slaves

Drinking Gourd: Big Dipper and the North Star

Flying bondsmen: The number of escaping slaves

Forwarding: Taking slaves from station to station

Freedom/Gospel Train: The Underground Railroad

Heaven: Canada, freedom

Stockholder: Those who donated money, food, clothing

Operator: Helped freedom seekers as a conductor or agent

Parcel: Fugitives that were expected

Patter roller: Bounty hunter hired to capture slaves

Promised Land: Canada

River Jordan: Ohio River

Shepherds: Encouraged slaves to escape and escorted them

Station: Place of safety and temporary refuge, a safe house

Stationmaster: Keeper or owner of a safe hous

Baptism, a staple of the faith, involves the immersion in water, and the symbolism is often used in the codes of songs such as "Wade in the Water." "Wade in the water, God's gonna trouble the water," for water would cover the scent of the slaveholders' bloodhounds tracking them. "If you don't believe I've been redeemed, follow me down to Jordan's stream"—or the Ohio River, where he or she would be free.

The line was also a dare to attempt to even try and get across the great river, because as Harriet Tubman said after her first failed escape with her brothers, "Freedom is only for the brave." "Follow the Drinkin' Gourd," also called "The Big Dipper," had a pointer—its alignment with the North Star. That led to the free states. Following it meant escape was in that direction, and it was God's own map at that. Better places waited for them after hearing songs like "Now Let Me Fly" because the Promised Land was only 100 or so miles north if they could get there—not in the "by and by." It gave them hope such a place existed and maybe "Ezekiel's wheels" could fly them there, even if that was as a "load of potatoes" behind a secret abolitionist's wagon.

Frederick Douglass and Harriet Tubman both escaped slavery and became autobiographers of their journey. They left us many recorded accounts of how these codes and terms were shared and used among them. They explain the secretive nature it had to have to save lives yet be used to spread the word for that reason also. Douglass wrote of the song's hidden messages:

"A keen observer might have detected in our repeated singing of 'O Canaan, sweet Canaan, I am bound for the land of Canaan' something more than a hope of reaching heaven. We meant to reach the north—and the north was our Canaan. I thought I heard them say, /There were lions in the way / I don't expect to stay / much longer here / was a favorite air and had a double meaning. In the lips of some, it meant the expectation of a speedy summons to a world of spirits; but in the lips of our company, it simply meant a speedy pilgrimage toward a free state, and deliverance from all the evils and dangers of slavery."

He was not unaware of how watched they all might have been:

"I am the more inclined to think that he suspected us, because ... we did many silly things, very well calculated to awaken suspicion."

If this is the case, while he represents the accounts of just his own experience like Harriet did of hers, these stories serve as at least some idea of how the practice of coding started. It did not free all the slaves, as no small, secret society like that could against the prevailing laws. However, they freed as many as they could this way—perhaps only a few hundred, perhaps less. However, the few like Douglass and Tubman who survived with their escape versions came from two different backgrounds; that might have been exactly how that took place in many other instances.

Knowing the coding in the song, the lyrics take on a new meaning for the listener:

Who's that yonder dressed in red?
Wade in the water
Must be the children that Moses led
And God's gonna trouble the water
Wade in the water

Wade in the water, children

Wade in the water

God's gonna trouble the water

    The songs used during the Underground Railroad were mostly the "safe" old Negro spirituals. What better way to tell them to get ready to run than–

Steal away ... steal away ... steal away to Jesus.

Steal away, steal away home! I ain't got long to stay here! My Lord calls me!

He calls me by the thunder!

The trumpet sound it in my soul! I ain't got long to stay here!

    Or that someone was out there waiting to help them on that Freedom Railroad by singing that a (sweet chariot) was coming south (swinging low) to take them north to freedom (carry me home). This was one of Tubman's favorite songs according to Sarah Hopkins Bradford's biography, Scenes in the Life of Harriet Tubman.

Swing low, sweet chariot, coming for to carry me home,

Swing low, sweet chariot, coming for to carry me home.

I looked over Jordan and what did I see

Coming for to carry me home,

A band of angels coming after me,

Coming for to carry me home.

If you get there before I do,

Coming for to carry me home,

Tell all my friends that I'm coming, too,

Coming for to carry me home.

Another unnamed song sung by Harriet when approaching her group after taking a detour to get food for the day to let them know it was safe to approach her went:

Hail, oh hail, ye happy spirits,

Death no more shall make you fear,

Grief nor sorrow, pain nor anguish,

Shall no more distress you there.

Around Him are ten thousand angels,

Always ready to obey command;

They are always hovering round you,

Till you reach the heavenly land.

Jesus, Jesus will go with you,

He will lead you to his throne;

He who died, has gone before you,

Through the wine-press all alone.

He whose thunders shake creation,

He who bids the planets roll;

He who rides upon the tempest,

And whose scepter sways the whole.

A song sang in the same situation but letting them know it was not safe to come out, there was danger in the way, was "Go Down, Moses" (a name by which Harriet was also called).

Chorus:

Oh, go down, Moses,

Way down into Egypt's land,

Tell old Pharaoh,

Let my people go.

Oh, Pharaoh said he would go cross,

Let my people go,

And don't get lost in the wilderness,

Let my people go.

You may hinder me here, but you can't up there,

Let my people go,

He sits in the Heaven and answers prayer,

Let my people go.

Indeed, music played a vital part in slaves finding their way north. Northern states had abolitionist cultures whose main goal was to help them reach Canada; no place in America was safe to them. There, American laws that allowed people to capture runaway slaves had no effect, unlike the places where returning escaped slaves as "rightful property" was encouraged. From hymns prescribed for finding Christ to spirituals passed around to find the north, the clever ways Africans got around their yoke were as innovative as the music that followed.

"What we play is life."

"You blows who you is."

"If ya ain't got it in ya, ya can't blow it out."

—*Louis Armstrong*

CHAPTER FOUR

CAPTURING THE TRUTH

After emancipation and the abolishment of slavery in 1865, schools like my own alma mater, Fisk University, opened their doors as did others like Tuskegee University. There, skills could be acquired so free Blacks could better assimilate. All the schools mentioned had their touring groups of Negro spiritual singers, who no doubt raised money as well as awareness of the schools and further education.

However, those songs reminded singers and audiences of those plantation days, and they began to regret making them so popular. Calling the music "the sole expression of Black life" was not the full truth, as those who were progressing with education, business, art, and politics wanted a place in society. No further reminders that they had once been white man's chattel were needed.

Laments to God were considered too sullen by the younger generation, now learning about the world, and so the sounds, lyrics, and energy behind the music changed. The worship factor remained, yet music branched out to distance them from olden days and sorrow that went with the songs.

It was in the sanctified and holiness churches that emerged after slavery close to the end of the century where this change was most seen. These spirited services, more than any others, reflected the traditional African customs that utilized music and the shouting praise styles that influenced them.

It got them roused even before emancipation talk came, and the liberated spirit made them long to be free. Once they were emancipated by law yet faced all the remaining hatred and discrimination Americans still held for them, that too became reflected in the music as it stretched beyond the fields and church walls. Starting in the 1880s in the earliest recordings, there were only traces of that "homegrown" authenticity music recorders were trying to capture: a sound originating from plantation work.

Yet the process of recording what included railroad construction songs and chain gang–type forced labor was unsuccessful because of a loss of authenticity from "staging" the music. The rapid-fire cadence that came from hardworking men laying and unloading steel rails, tie-shuffling, and tie-tamping chants was indicative of the atmosphere and energy of the task. I can hardly imagine they were easy to reproduce under the sterile settings of an early recording setup.

Some songs were collected and compiled in American Ballads and Folk Songs by John A. Lomax, Alan Lomax, and Ruth Crawford Seeger, music editor, in 1941. In 1995, Alan Lomax published The Land Where the Blues Began, which emphasized how segregated, forced laborers, sharecroppers, and those still living under the guise of slavery gave birth to the blues. Lomax published the book after spending years, like his folklorist father John A. Lomax before him, collecting and preserving by recording much of the blues, folk, and even original work songs throughout the nation, including the south and as far as Europe. He was credited with the discovery of guitarist Robert Johnson, a blues legend, and Leadbelly, who reigned in both blues and country. By casting his net far and wide, he could bring to the forefront other names in folk and country genres as well, such as Pete Seeger and Woody Guthrie who lent his voice to the protest movement.

The music, his interviews, and the earliest examples of what those field workers' songs sounded like were all preserved on aluminum disks for all time at the Archive of American Folk Song/Library of Congress, where Lomax was also a director.

Up from the sorrow songs or spirituals on into the blues, the sound would continue to evolve with each generational spin on it and based on the energy of the times. By the time the 1920s rolled in, continuing into the '40s, Race Records hit phonographs at 78 rpm and took Black American genres across the world. By then, gospel, jazz, blues, and even Black comedy records could be found, bringing the earlier generations' music forward with little improvisation. Those first releases would have greatly authenticated Black experiences in the post–Civil War through Reconstruction periods, as many were recorded by offspring of former slaves.

The music was infectious, as is any great song when played loud and often enough, and Black listeners found they were not alone in acquiring the Race Records as white audiences gradually jumped on the bandwagon. Billboard published a Race Records chart between 1945 and 1949, initially covering jukebox plays, and from 1948, also covering sales.

This was a revision of the Harlem Hit Parade chart, presented first in 1942. Just as the names for the people and their music evolved, so did Billboard's charts: from Rhythm & Blues Records to the soul chart in 1969, to the Black chart in 1982, and again the R&B chart in 1990, before becoming the R&B/hip-hop chart in 1999. Before these transitions, in the time just after the Civil War, it is significant in tracing Black music to see how it worked as a means for further freeing up lives economically. Often, they would take jobs as musicians. The Black church employed preachers who were often musicians themselves. Whether a drummer in the military band, playing ragtime for fancy establishments and parties for the wealthy, nightclubs, recordings, and tours as far as Europe, they filled the hole of poverty.

Playing in so many places, joining in with instrumentalists and composers from around the country, and adapting components they learned along the way, musicians pushed the music to new heights, and the popularity grew.

Some did make money, like comedian/musician Moms Mabley, who reigned in her field. She, as well as blues legend Bessie Smith, was known to have made tremendous revenue compared to most Black women and even other entertainers of their time. They had immense appeal to white and Black audiences once both hit early films, such as Smith in St. Louis Blues, and Mabley on into television in the late '80s. Moms Mabley ruled the charts with her songs. Their fame lasts even now.

However, compared to what was coming in worldwide, future royalties, and the amount of control had by the labels, most artists then, like today, made a pittance in comparison.

When European instruments, waltzes, baroque, and classical styles met Africans brought over to America, the combination was much like what the captives in New Orleans created in their gumbos—taking whatever was on hand and making it sing. The misery of slavery, the pain of homesickness, the limitations on their humanity all flavored their sound, just as it did all their art.

Beatboxing, spoken word, jazz scatting, and rapping today can find their roots in field hollers and call and responses from the plantations of slaveholding America. From blues to boogie-woogie and bebop, early sounds borrowed on the atmosphere, just as hip-hop and rap do today.

The instrumentations from early jug bands and on into ragtime and even jazz also evolved with the vocalizations in music to go as far as doo-wop, funk, disco, and today's synthesized sounds behind house and hip-hop. Music such as go-go, like some house music, uses the drum sounds and heavy percussion indicative of the influences of African rhythms.

Standing out in the recording done by the Lomaxes was "Hammer Ring," which was sung by Jesse Bradley in 1934 with a group at the state penitentiary in Huntsville, Texas. John A. Lomax wrote of the action behind the song, "Gandy Dancers."

"The men who drove the spikes that fastened the long steel rails to the wooden ties sang the most thrilling tune of all—the hammer song, song of the ten-pound hammer with its two heads scarcely more than a couple of inches in diameter, that was swung free from the shoulder in a

complete circle about the head ... that song with its own individual vibrant and stirring tune."

To give context to the hard labor these songs accompanied, one needs an idea of the type of work being done. A tamping machine or ballast tamper packs/tamps the ballast under railway tracks for better track durability. Before the machines, this was done by men beating them with the sounds of—

Tamp 'em up solid, all the livelong day.

Tamp 'em up solid,

Then they'll hold that midnight mail.

The captain don't like me.

Won't allow me no show.

Well, work don't hurt me,

Don't care where in the world I go.

Work don't hurt me,

Like the early rise,

Well, work don't hurt me,

But that's the thing that hurts my pride,

That hurts my pride ...

Two such songs were recorded in 1939: "Quittin' Time Songs I & II" by Samuel Brooks and "Arwhoolie (Cornfield Holler)" sung by Thomas J. Marshall. Both were students at the Southern Christian Institute, Mount Beulah College, in Edwards, Mississippi. Having been raised together from childhood, they also worked together and could perform the original songs. If you listen to some of the earliest recordings, the work songs have the underpinnings of the raw sound of blues music, one of the most poignant forms of crooning known to man. By using their art forms to blend into the new society, and to strengthen them during the forced tasks, they could reclaim a sense of identity even through generations of subjugation. Later, that same art was used for stirring revolution and celebrating liberation.

By taking Christian hymns and texts and reinterpreting them using traditional African ideology, music couldn't help but morph into something before that unheard.

Dancing and movement to "the spirit" is a factor that made Black reinterpretation of the white Christian church's versions of the songs. Much hand clapping, foot shuffling, and danced-out energized praise (or "shout" as it was called) went into spirituals, so that even those listening "got the spirit." Increasing the tempo and adding more percussive sounds and instrumentation made the beginnings of that famous Black church gospel music. If they were going to spread the good news, the music helped to do it loud.

The sense of spiritual fervor got thicker by the 1830s in America, and Christian faith was at an all-time high among all the believers—even in the slave-held community. With the devotion came the music and, with so much created and copied, it passed plantation to plantation when the neighboring ones would gather for events (barn raisings, weddings, funerals, and holidays).

In praise and celebration, the music had its own special place and meaning, yet it could also hold a message—a secret one if needed. When planning to leave the plantation, it would prove to be the safest means to carry it.

It was also in this era that the historically Black (although founded by a white religious establishment) Fisk University introduced the Fisk University Jubilee Singers, who were key in spreading music via their tours beginning in 1871 and continued by a new generation today.

The five former slaves in the group saved the financially failing university with their rich musical gifts. The money made singing across the country not only helped the school, it built the platform for other Black touring groups to be welcomed across America in the years to follow.

Black comedy (like dance and art) was always near and neatly tucked behind many artists' performances. Professional acts like the comedy troupe The Hyers Sisters Comic Opera Co. combined music and laughter for their audiences as early as 1876. In the Black community, gathering places such as churches, cookouts, house parties, storefronts, and even barbershops and funeral homes met the needs for spreading news, information, and music. Mostly men (often musically raised) would come together in barbershops and funeral homes, and the development of a song would come about naturally.

It continued to be a unified effort to make songs, and from the harmonies and rhythms came the early barbershop quartets within social atmospheres. By the time white minstrelsy took it on, commercialization of it had occurred, along with freewill use of songs and styles by popular white singers.

Too much fun during work was frowned upon by plantation owners; therefore, most of the songs were somber and sad, displaying emotions of disappointment and defeat to the untrained ear. One thing Black Americans must be given credit for is the trick of hidden messaging and coding.

Not just a guide to get north but a rulebook on how to get by, face the oppressor, and make fun or shed light, music could be used to free a thought, a dream, and even anger, yet be so cloaked the foreman might just nod along, unaware.

At times, foremen who worked for the plantation owners would encourage singing to keep workers focused on the job at hand as well as keeping an accurate account of every hand on deck by the voices heard in unison. In this way, those songs that were eventually recorded by the Lomax outfit and others later were essentially ongoing rehearsals for what was to come. A lot of what developed as the early music heard in the fields and churches, and later recorded, came out of the scant leisure time slaves had as chances for mingling and mixing with slaves from other plantations. This was not necessarily a time for fun as much as it would theoretically ease their idea of the ongoing workload in the master's eyes.

Instead, the time was filled with other neglected duties, necessary in maintaining their own livelihood, things such as washing clothes and cooking their own family's meals. Since reading, writing, and math, etc., were strictly subjects studied by the masters' children, the African style of passing on messages, news, gossip, jokes, and praise was through songs.

Once sharecropping replaced the institution of slavery, the same demanding schedules and lack of real leisure and community time would make precious the Sunday services, the circle dances, and the socials they did have.

There, the music that reminded them of their parents and grandparents, of homelands distant but somehow still lying under the beat, came out and then began spreading. Certain songs and melodies were catchy, even among the white land-owning fiddlers and banjo players, who had begun to let that "spice and flavor" seep into some of their music just as it had into their southern cuisine.

Passing ears, enterprising minds such as the Lomaxes, even as early as the late 1800s, knew there was a magical and yet undeniable quality of pain in that sound that came from former slaves. They were industrious enough with the early recording equipment to go and find the rare and unique voices that could still evoke that plantation sound—before it faded with the turn of the century.

Had they not, we wouldn't have "Arhoolie" or the tie-tamping songs like it that were captured in those days, and although they lack that authentic sound they might have been looking for, it preserved a piece of heritage that bridges today's blues and other genres with its true roots.

Once emancipated, the free Black community had to rely on skills, wits, and sense of community to survive the next level of white America's rules and regulations for society. The performer may have lived a ragtag life, playing and getting paid sporadically, with few profits from any other labor in between.

The nineteenth century offered a new form of entertainment: minstrel shows. These shows were first a product of white performers in burnt cork-face portrayals of stereotyped Black life, then real Black artists also in blackface, all with similar styles of routines. Here the banjo took hold as the backing sound of those shows, and many of the songs utilized its sound.

Blackface performers are " ... *the filthy scum of white society, who have stolen from us a complexion denied them by nature, in which to make money, and pander to the corrupt taste of their white fellow citizens."*
—*Frederick Douglass*

CHAPTER FIVE

WHO WEARS THE MASK?

Blackface was supposed to be a caricature of real Black people. Instead, it was often a derogatory poke at them and their traditions and physiques, often grossly exaggerated for comedic effect. As hugely popular as it became during the nineteenth century, the only purpose it truly served was to keep free Blacks in their places and to reinforce racial stereotypes as a form of white superiority. The frolicking, joyful, "happy-to-be here!" Black dancer could be called a "coon" or a "darky" with openness in minstrel shows, and nobody batted an eye.

By the time actual Black performers took it on as a form of employment around the 1840s, it was more a matter of trying to slip in their true artistry. By singing, playing instruments, and dancing, it motivated them—not only for pay; they hoped their genuine talents could have a chance to ease audiences away from those loudly called-for stereotypes.

In the 1800s, traveling shows were the only way for people with products to sell—whether that product was a song, some snake oil, or a show—to reach buyers. The circuses and musical hall troupes traveled everywhere to entertain and make cash sales. Soon everyone who could form an act jumped in. Jim Crow's horrendous era was seeded by the mockery created by Thomas Dartmouth "Daddy" Rice, who was considered the Father of American Minstrelsy. His performances in the late 1820s included a ragtag blackface characterization using a common plantation song, "Jump Jim Crow." It was based on trickster symbols found in plantation folklore.

Using spoons, banjos, brass and bone castanets, tambourines, and fiddles, the Virginia Minstrels started the earliest examples of minstrel shows in 1843. By the time they were popular, there was a three-part routine heavy with plantation/slave dialects and characters doing skits and traditional songs. The routine began in a company march, dancing around a song, toward the stage in what was called a walkaround. The irony was that the show favorite—the cakewalk—was a dance made to mock Western European customs, including how they walked.

After hitting the stage, they gathered in a U-shaped half circle facing the audience. One trouper plays the tambourine on one end (always named Brother Tambo and usually large) and, on the other side, another endman (Brother Bones, who was typically skinny) tosses jokes back and forth in a series of skits and dances. The character Mr. Interlocutor is the middleman and master of ceremonies, who always delivers the same opening line, "Gentlemen, be seated. We will commence with the overture." He plays the straight man to the other players' antics.

The routines shifted but the blackface stayed the course. You simply must watch the 1977 movie with Glynn Turman, Minstrel Man, if you want a riveting portrayal of not just the lives these performers led but the racial pressure they faced while doing it.

To make life for the abolitionists that much harder, the minstrel shows gave pre-Civil War pro-slavery advocates a way of keeping the image of the inferior Negro alive. It served their narrative of slavery being a more useful tool for civilizing slaves. By showing them frolicking and grinning around in some happy-go-lucky shuffle, they tried to reinforce that nothing bad was happening to them.

They're not complaining, they're dancing and singing —that was the message behind the shows.

Even after the captives were emancipated, the same themes continued because Lincoln's law of no law, the mask of blackness as seen by the slaveholding community was fixed and needed to be lest they lose their own position seated above them.

The minstrels introduced many techniques that caught on and spread, like tap dancing and hambonin'. However, there was little room to add improvisation in early minstrel shows because the image of the stereotype was central to the show, and that included the spirituals and other music thought of as "slave songs." The men behind the characters adopted all the roles, including the women, such as minstrel show favorite "Miss Lucy Long," popular in the 1840s, with many other troupes developing their own female impersonations.

Stephen Foster, the songwriter behind the most mainstream tunes in the mid- and late-1800s, regretted the lack of serious consideration given to his musicianship and talent and had his greater abilities trivialized in the minstrel shows. This was often the case where "real" artists wanted to showcase their talents, but audiences wanted the bottom-of-the-barrel stuff.

By the twentieth century, minstrel shows with blackface were an institution and a precursor to the "chitlin circuit" era of performers that ran the poor, mostly Black, nightclub routes on into the late '70s. The BBC's "The Black and White Minstrel Show" ran as late as 1978 to over eighteen million TV watchers, who made it the most popular and best-known minstrel show in the world.

The changes in attitude by the time the civil rights movement of the 1960s emerged offered the Black community a relief from the widespread, by then, television antics of what was supposed to be more refined and politically correct primetime parody of Black life.

By the end of the 1970s, rare shows with actual Black performers such as "Amos 'n' Andy" were frowned upon and being increasingly boycotted as racially degrading.

Those white pioneers of blackface thought their burnt-cork or shoe-polished blackness, alongside those songs they heard growing up from the Black laborers, would not only be funny but profitable. Wool for hair and exaggerated lips gave them a show, but it was a role they could never understand—being Black. There was no humanity in "coon songs," and the spirituals they adopted were hollow versions of the "spirit" that led to their creations on plantations by stolen Africans.

Frederick Douglass wrote vehemently about blackface and rightly pointed to its beginnings among northern whites trying to profit off it, yet adding that at least there was something in Black men being allowed to appear before a white audience.

Being that these were often freed slaves, the blackface minstrel shows were promoted as such and were supposed to rival the white acts by being authentically Black.

Yet the reactions were more spectator, like when white audiences came to gawk at them for their "exotic" or "animalistic" reputations. The talents and songs were then buried under much misunderstanding and pre-conceived prejudices.

These Colored Troupes, as they were called, attempted to evolve the art form by straying away from stereotypes and politically charged themes. This allowed them to focus on the music and not stir the prejudice of the audience with the same material the white performers used in minstrelsy.

With what was supposed to represent true plantation music and reenactments, the Georgia Minstrels—put on in 1866 by the duo Booker and Clayton—became hugely popular. Being given the rare chance for towns to get live entertainment—even of the minstrel variety—would have been a special occasion.

Dances from plantation life, like the hambone or "hambonin'" and the patting juba, using just feet, hands, and clapping/shuffling motions alone, survived on these stages and in that way.

What you see today grew up out of those, as each troupe and mimicker of it adapted the style. Another group called Sam Hague's Slave Troupe of Georgia Minstrels grew popular enough to tour overseas before it changed over to Haverly's Colored Minstrels.

Bert Williams and George Walker

Once the real Black performers mastered the genre, white troupes moved on from blackface subjects; without their continued reinforcement of the negative imagery, troupes could further evolve it.

It was the Fisk Jubilee Singers and their rousing mix of spirituals, and even some other aspects of ever-morphing Black church music, that helped advance those minstrel troupes past those stages. By inspiring less "plantation" material for audiences, they forced listeners to hear the changes taking place in the Black community now that freedom and a better life seemed possible.

The sound of their unity was reflective of how the community was beginning to use the church and its message to implant broader ones with the music being the vessel. The people listened and, without the filters of negatively portrayed performers representing a limited perspective of their potential, freed Black Americans found a voice by the 1970s.

Self-directed parody was not unwelcomed in the shows Black performers gave; it was not the same variety of "fun" the white audiences got out of racially derogatory imaging. The burnt-corkface routines were an acceptable form of delivering material at the time, and so they used it, no matter that they were Black. It was the only way they were allowed on stage. The mask of blackness was desired by the white audience, covering the genuine talents and abilities of the Black performer beneath it.

To make jest of the situation for any artists had to happen. Whatever salaries, large or meager, that the Black minstrel performers earned, it fed them. If the conventional attitudes of the day were to hide their blackness behind the black of greasepaint, then so be it—for a while. It would seem the minstrel performers who rose out of that and into other forms of entertainment, later shaping vaudeville and other style shows, were always pushing boundaries to get away with more each generation.

The buffoonery was called for, but it tempered into comedy. Today's comics who turn the lens around to view Black life with self-parody are inheritors of that tradition through minstrelsy and vaudeville. A Black man or woman couldn't even speak without being in costume, much less tell a joke, as some of the more racist audience members felt. It was easier to use jokes—subtle turnabouts where it was the white audience who was the joke—and slip in as much raw, unstoppable talent as they could hold.

The Black audiences understood and made these performing troupes and jubilee singers, now grown in number, celebrated acts. As stars of their community in grassroots ways, upper-crust members of Black society and its academia kin were not keen on it at all. Condemned from the depths of their intellectual understandings, the protestation to end minstrelsy was loud.

Just as rap music entered with its strong opponents who thought it misrepresented the growth and progress of Black Americans, so did other early forms of entertainment that did not meet a structured guideline of dignity. It so echoes the abolitionist's guidance of behavior during slavery for former captives who managed to gain freedom but were forced to still live in a white society.

Scholars like Booker T. Washington had once advised that when one's head was in the lion's mouth, he should pet it. Opponents like W. E. B. DuBois thought that was ridiculous and had more aggressive opinions about handling white society's notions, but neither side argued for the continuation of blackface parody. Yet most had to admire its ability to open doors, bring newer financial opportunities for underemployed sectors of the Black community, and provide a platform for them before white people that had never existed. They were throwing the baby out with the bathwater when they condemned it, but much of it (mostly whites in blackface) was so damaging to a progressive Black person that it needed to be.

It's important to see that the music and performance it offered for Black minstrels was in its way liberating. Instead of the railroad tamping jobs, porter work, janitorial or groundskeeper jobs, and backbreaking work the former slaveholders offered, they had their talents. When they made their first pay off it and fed the family, what a marvel it must have seemed to others scraping for a living off former plantation skills!

"Corking up" for cash must have been a wonder to a man who could play no instruments, sing not one note, nor dance to anybody's liking.

Black audiences got a chance to see at least some of the positive aspects, hear the traditional and innovated music, and participate in something that once again drew them all together: those shows. They were seeing themselves in any form, given the window into how we were pushing those boundaries as each joke changed into one slightly more empowering than the last.

A chance to wag a comic finger at racist white Americans in the southern states was permissible in its subtlest forms, if hid in the right song or skit. A way to lampoon white folks and get them to laugh at themselves was a strike back at them using the stage—the one platform they were given. Satire in their comedy—poking fun with a dance like the "cakewalk" caricaturing white customs—allowed a liberating chance to speak back.

After centuries of no voice, stifled down in "laughing barrels" where a joke had to be stuffed if an offended southern white man happened to not be in the mood, why not take a stage and talk back? If it was carefully cloaked, blacked up darker than the performer would ever be, it might pass and even pay.

In 1909, the Theater Owners Booking Association (TOBA) headlined all the major Black talent on the all-Black vaudeville circuit. Because the work was so hard, the circuit so racist and rough, and all for pay that was a pittance, it was also famously called "Tough on Black Artists." Even so, it beat field labor, sharecropping, chain gangs, and tar-paper shack lives waiting for them otherwise.

The same Apollo Theater in Harlem stages that performers hit today has featured talents and acts from the 1930s and '40s vaudeville and chitlin circuits, even when performers were still sporting blackface. Protested nonetheless, it was deeply ingrained in the way performers could present themselves; how easy would it have been to change the whole show? If it wasn't broken and was making them a living, why fix it? The NAACP or anybody else would find it hard to work those habits out of blackface performers, even into the civil rights era's beginnings. A great way to sum up the general understanding of the entire art form, where musical gifts meet socio-political walls, was given by dramatist/poet/essayist Amiri Baraka (a.k.a. LeRoi

Jones) when he wrote, "It is essential to realize that ... the idea of white men imitating, or caricaturing, what they consider certain generic characteristics of the Black man's life in America is important if only because of the Negro's reaction to it. (And it is the Negro's reaction to America, first white and then Black and white America, that I consider to have made him such a unique member of this society). ..."

Those talented Black musicians who did break through to the mainstream redefined the genres they touched, and it would be but a matter of time before they took over where they could. On Broadway, as early as 1898, Black musicians were writing and producing musicals, such as Billy Johnson and Bob Cole, who debuted their works on the Great White Way.

By the 1930s, Broadway was still showcasing blackface imagery too, although it eventually evolved over the years with the advancement of Black entertainment.

This happened to coincide with the growth in social positioning by the men and women behind the art form, making it, by the end of the nineteenth century, an established aspect of mainstream American culture.

Live performance opened the door in 1901 with the Slayton Jubilee Singers, as in that same year, 1901, Bert Williams and George Walker brought Broadway musical opportunities. While the genres opened further with opera when the Drury Opera Company utilized Black performers in leading roles in 1900, it still featured an all-white orchestra. Until 1908, Theodore Drury ran the company that gave Black opera singers a stage upon which to expand their talents.

Always proving to be innovators in any field they touched, these early Black performers brought other elements with them, such as with the folksy-ragtime opera created by Scott Joplin, Treemonisha, in 1911. After World War II, the country's attitudes greatly shifted after having so many foreign enemies to deal with; some were tired of seeing them in their fellow citizens at home in America.

The changes happened as both the music and its exposure to white audiences increased and after Black soldiers had also been exposed to more progressive mindsets in Europe. European audiences and citizens had no problems accepting jazz, gospel, blues, ragtime, and any other art form, and it mattered not that a Black artist was behind it. Such acceptance opened the way for bolder actions on behalf of protestors, community leaders, and even musicians back home.

Once the areas of electronic delivery of radio and recording expanded, and major influences such as the collectives of artists in Philadelphia and in Harlem with their respective renaissances were felt, the music spread further and gained open supporters even in white households—especially with jazz.

Jazz did more to bridge the gaps between young white music lovers and Black activists than just about any other genre. Jazz music was the cause of many an argument in a wealthy Jewish or Anglo-Saxon household during that era.

Persisting nonetheless, the musicians themselves would often let anyone—white or Black—join in a jam session. The vibe allowed mixing of men and women and the chance to date one another; under the spell of the seductive atmosphere of a New York jazz club, this mingling became all too common.

Even while improvising on the European classical sounds, early Black musicians around the turn of the twentieth century also mastered symphony orchestration as well. Both the Oberlin School of Music and the New England Conservatory, as well as the National Conservatory of Music, offered study programs for Black musicians. Black-led orchestras increased in the early 1900s across the country. By the 1910s, the all-Black music schools Martin-Smith School of Music and the Music School Settlement for Colored were founded in New York.

The 1920s were chock-full of musical theatre acts that took over Broadway, including Shuffle Along, which introduced the world to Josephine Baker. The 1921 Noble Sissle and Eubie Blake musical is one of the most famous, launching numerous careers to mainstream music platforms.

People who had grown up dirt poor and uncounted by society, like Josephine Baker in her childhood, found not just worldwide fame but massive fortunes that allowed them to move to Europe and forget those lives.

Viewers got film productions like King Vidor's 1929 Hallelujah and similar ones created to showcase the booming talents of artists like Paul Robeson, alongside all-Black operas like Porgy and Bess, as they filled major venues like Carnegie Hall.

In the 1920s, a new creative energy took place in the form of a Black Renaissance artist movement. By taking the components of music and even poetry, they refined the songs, such as by removing patois or southern Black dialect. By offering the music—even as Negro spirituals but cleaned of the dialects—the more educated Blacks felt this would broaden the growth of the people as well. Strong southern phrases and accents like "Lawd" instead of "Lord," for example, might have been edited for mainstream consumption and the artists encouraged to be more educated.

This constant improvement of Black music has not only kept the people in the game, it has kept the ever-copied styles a source for connecting all racial groups worldwide.

By the time Blacks left the south, northern cities adopted the gospel songs that grew up out of the old spirituals, with songwriters like Thomas Dorsey, called the Father of Gospel Music. While R&B, jazz, rock, and even pop have traveled and changed over time, gospel has also, but it has always ridden its own distinct lane and kept a devoted audience despite the changing times.

It endures as untampered-with remnants of the old sound of heartfelt supplications, both to God and to our fellow man for a better life. It spoke then and still speaks for the spirits ever climbing out of misery and seeking freedom for body, mind, and soul.

When it comes to instrumentation, orchestras led by the New York Philharmonic and the Afro-American Symphony proliferated in the 1930s, as Black musicians showed their mastery of every instrument in use.

With so much growth in Black music, and after having bowed out of the blackface game, what were white musicians doing with the popularity of the Black music sound? Covers. Lots of them. Those covers of Black artists' material would top the charts, and their faces on the music's sleeves would reassure racist buyers it was "white music with flavor. The mainstream money did not trickle down, and the practice took hold into the twenty-first century.

Black artists innovated again, because it seems staying one step ahead of the game was the only way to keep the feeling of "liberation" and freedom in their music. Keeping the lanes original and clear of outside control was as much a part of a Black artist's life as was his life in a former slaveholding society.

By the '40s and '50s, rock and roll was a sound that R&B singers had begun playing with. Black musicians had time to do this, having already revolutionized instrumentation and musical improvisations in jazz, with masters like Miles Davis, John Coltrane, Dizzy Gillespie, and others having set the bar far above many heads. The influencer of country music and R&B artists alike was Sister Rosetta Tharpe, whose original songs were everything early rock music grew into.

Little Richard would agree, having also credited her influence in his music. Elvis Presley took the popular crown, along with other white artists, and Sister Tharpe is a forgotten footnote to a genre she so greatly shaped.

That left Black artists to land on their musical feet again with something even newer—doo-wop, using harmonics of voice and scatting stutter of melody around common lyrics. Vocalists then had the chance to stand out individually, even while being backed by a group, with special soloists taking center stage and crooning crowds to their knees.

Most of the prominent names who came out from the 1940s on came up out of gospel or R&B groups—from Mahalia Jackson to Sam Cooke. Their upbringing in the church is what developed the "soul" sound that flipped all the genres on their sides when applied to any style of singing—such as Ray Charles on a Cole Porter ballad or Aretha Franklin on a Broadway tune.

By the time white doo-wop groups had TV for their platforms, with whole TV shows formed around them, Berry Gordy and his family were pulling together what would be the most revolutionary element to all music for generations to come: Motown Records. By taking poor artists from their inner-city neighbors and honing their talents in artists' development and refinement courses, Gordy took soul, R&B, pop, gospel, and every other genre and wrapped them around every vocalist the label ever worked with.

Their versatility and dexterity with songs show the success of his guiding their skills into the mainstream market. For the first time, perhaps ever in record industry marketing, a Black leader took control and his records sold into the millions uncontrolled. Gospel had its stars as well, and their tours swelled church congregations across the nation, selling as many records as any other genre.

The sound of it came on the cusp of revolution. The advent of the transistor radio made music portable. Having

Diana, Marvin, the Four Tops, or the Temptations in your pocket and closer to your ear was a reminder of the power of music. It motivated and galvanized when the Temptations sang about living on "Cloud Nine" and "Ball of Confusion."

As decades passed, music led listeners in the Black community to even more outspoken artists. From as early as the 1950s, Black pride music and resistance songs had begun to take hold. With white supporters of the music and patrons of Black arts, the movement could be better financed and exposed to the mainstream. James Brown, Nina Simone, and other names resonated as announcers of the power of not just Black music but its people.

In the UK, British artists caught the flavor and liberally sprinkled Wilson Pickett and other artists' sounds into their boy band sounds; every subgenre started tasting it in theirs. Crossover success from Motown artists gave way to others being embraced, even down to the more obscure and previously unrecorded artists who enjoyed renewed attention as the last of their authentic-sounding eras. Europe and the theatre eagerly employed these talents from the vaudeville era, who still carried some of the "old style" and a repertoire of early Black music favorites.

Always ahead of the curve, instruments also took on new innovations by Black artists like Jimi Hendrix. Using new technology of the times, his feedback was food for hungry audiences looking for more and more effect in performance. What he could do with a "wah wah" pedal made for 1960s psychedelic culture. The fuzz of his guitar's screams matched much of the audience's as drugs and more liberal lifestyles made for wilder crowds.

The pulse of revolution touched every youth group, whether about war or politics, and racial relations was a hot-button topic; why wouldn't the music reflect it?

Open minds paved the way for mainstream success, like the 1970s hits from Marvin Gaye on What's Going On. People were ready to hear about America's issues and the poignant delivery of it by a major headliner such as Gaye delivered hit the right tone and the correct time. Fellow label-mate Stevie Wonder put together perfectly the spiritual and intellectual accuracy of how far Black America had come in Songs in the Key of Life.

Soul took hold into the 1970s. The dragged-out Vietnam War had worn out and killed off so many vibrant young people. Badly needed was more Motown, a label that always knew how to roll with the times, adding the harder, instrument-heavy fusions called funk.

Groups who brought the sound made party music out of any theme, and moving the body to the beat was as necessary as ever. The innovation of dances had always evolved with the songs, starting at some house party and the next minute introduced on "Bandstand" with Dick Clark. Black dance was as widespread as its music in every era. Funk music gave that pulsating sound that brought about another type of unity—on the dance floor.

Sly & The Family Stone made a pop-soul fusion of their own out of it that defied anything before it. George Clinton later came along and colored it with something altogether more psychedelic. P-funk was as popular as the growing sound coming from the radios by the mid-'70s, a sound called disco. If Donna Summer was any indication, Black purveyors of the sound could do no wrong to the white mainstream, just as she was embraced by her own. Disco was another genre to bridge many gaps, allowing for the mingling of races and defying conventions of the time. Open mixed marriages and changes in social norms made the music a common denominator in many communities, where integrated living and schooling was beginning to take place.

Racial prejudices and limitations, extreme poverty, and more of the same as the olden days still existed in the south for Blacks, but paths had cleared, and music had been one of the tools used to do so.

The freedoms gained, such as ridding society of Jim Crow laws, colored-only signs, and limits in education were apparent, but not nearly as far along as needed. Yet music had built bridges in communication, and once the urgency of their causes could be heard, even if under the melodic cries of the blues, more people listened.

In New York, when the end of the 1960s brought the sounds of MCs and DJs running albums on extended play between turntables, another sound was born. Having a wealth of material through the '70s, from James Brown's "Funky Drummer" to other classics, the MCs could talk over them and hype up the crowd. Just as the leader in the group of workers called for a response, and like the circles of dancers and chanters in those plantation dances, were those breakdancing and rap "cyphers" where they circled around together. The beats, the hand claps, the dances, and the "griot" rapper delivering the word of the day—in rhythm.

Not much had changed as far as traditional unified performances and ways of rousing a group.

Hip-hop drew openly on the Universal Zulu Nation's concepts of African influence, and the basic components of the art form were always breakdancing (b-boying), graffiti art, MCing (chanting/rapping/rhyming/orating), DJing (instrumentation only using the music spun from turntables for the beats). This last innovation has overtaken mainstream music as we know it. "As of 2017 the billion-dollar genre surpasses all others in sales worldwide. R&B/hip-hop music was the year's biggest genre, accounting for 24.5 percent of all music consumed. According to Nielsen Music, total music consumption in the US in 2017" (Billboard, 2017)

Hip-hop has overtaken music lovers around the world, with a rapper for every country there is, in every racial group. It has diversified all other genres with its influence and has itself split into numerous subgenres over the last three decades. On its heels, R&B, neo-soul, Black alternative, and even African American innovations in pop have made for multi-million mainstream success, even for the artists.

With all the wealth gained, awareness of the source of the soul does not go unnoticed by contemporary artists. The lessons on from where we as a country have come since the heinous era of slavery is always a footnote to our more conscientiously written music.

"Without New Orleans' rich musical contribution there would have been no Elvis Presley or The Beatles. Both acts were heavily influenced by the songs recorded by Fats Domino and Little Richards at Cosimo Matassa's Studios (close to Congo Square)."

— Fabian Jolivet

CHAPTER SIX

SYNCOPATIONS & INNOVATIONS

The African American Performers on Early Sound Recordings, 1892-1916, is an interesting collection you can research online and get a good understanding of just that. These were not "big names" of the times—rather men and women gathered by talent scouts more so for what their voices brought with them: the songs, the lyrics.

Sure, money came in from Race Records and Black artists selling and performing, but those songs in the mouths of the more popularly accepted white artists was even better. It makes sense if they were only going to slap an image of a white performer on a Black singer's record anyway. Once they had a handful of white artists who could get down the sound, it still left the authenticity that came from the poignancy of the lyrics and melodies.

Those early 1890s recordings are of a time when Black artists rarely performed on early recordings. It was the exception to the rule that Black artists sold his or her songs. It was someone's job to take raw talent and teach them how to record in those early days, using equipment that would look medieval to today's producers. A large horn took in sound, and the field hollers alone must have blasted. Trained in diction and delivery by recruiters, the recording techniques got better, and early companies sprang up with more professionally trained (read white artists here also) artists who could deliver the oldies like the best.

Those early names in recording that you find in the archives like Bert Williams and George Walker, who released songs like "Her Name's Miss Dinah Fair," found success with both white and Black audiences, but most others could be replaced over time. Walker and Williams had the chops to place the poshest New York vaudeville houses, so, naturally, anything they recorded was going to sell better—and under their own names.

For most other raw talent from off the streets or fields from down south, their lack of training in a studio hurt their chances to get further. They could rock a church revival tent full of parishioners with no microphone, but it somehow didn't translate over wax. Professional reorders became the order of the day for a while and squeezed out Black talent from that profit pool.

The first commercially released song with a Black artist was in 1890, albeit many of them were done in "a coon manner" according to the popularity of the times. The first, "The Laughing Song," was recorded by a former slave, George W. Johnson. He was recruited by a Berliner agent, who for some reason created a sea of myths around both his discovery and his life and released that song with his picture on it—rare for the times. He was later to release more songs under Berliner, Edison, and Columbia.

That same year, the Unique Quartette also recorded as well, as in subsequent years, a string of songs which survive in the archives collection as one of the clearest examples of recordings of that era. With fifteen recordings between them and some of those as solos, the William and Walker team found their own success with the Victor Talking Machine Company. This company took a rare and bolder approach of promoting their Black talent in those early days. Whether it was the comedy of George W. Johnson or, later, the Fisk University Jubilee Singers, by 1909 their label's artists had advertisements running across the nation.

Making the disks we have today, in aluminum or acetate, was a complicated process that didn't always yield sound results. The stampers that pressed them would wear out and sessions would have to be constantly rerecorded. If performers were on the road touring, which most did for their bread and butter, it became difficult for labels like Victor to get the best full recordings. That is why what we have today are so rare. Further, those like George Walker, who didn't like his recorded voice, may have begun to avoid the recording process for that reason, especially if the artist had popular live appearances to make up the difference in income.

After 1911, the performer could finally have his rightful place alongside the song in mainstream music, as Bert Williams proved after the death of his partner, George Walker. Williams joined the popular Ziegfeld Follies and then went on to become one of Columbia Records' biggest early stars with top-selling power. Many others in the Black music community had a popular hold on the audiences; however, those were not recorded and did not find their way into the recorded material.

Yet the songs they composed and the musical stylings were adapted by white vocalists and reinterpreted for their own continued parodying of Black life, such as the interpretation remix done on Hogan's song, "All Coons Look

Alike to Me," rerecorded by a performer named Arthur Collins for Edison Company.

"Under the Bamboo Tree" was a type of "coon" song that utilized full dialect as a signature of popular artists like Collins, who proved to be one of the most prolific recording artists around the turn of the century. Many compositions did get the stereotyping treatment while a few others were handled respectfully and rerecorded by white artists for the Edison Company, such as J. Leubrie Hill's "At the Ball That's All."

The most successful songwriters that forged their own careers out of vaudeville were J. Rosamond Johnson, her notable brother James Weldon Johnson, and writer Bob Cole. With a sophistication to their act, they removed all signs of racial stereotyping and buffoonery and offered classy dress and a refined performance.

In a 1922 record by the New Orleans Rhythm Kings (NORK), creative techniques and instrumental harmonies and rhythms kicked off the style of reinterpretation song that would gain long-term wings as did "Panama," a traditional jazz favorite. W. C. Handy had a version that offers a look at the original rearrangements that made it such a standout in early jazz inspiration.

Detroit musician Fred S. Stone also recorded for Edison in 1900 with "Ma Ragtime Baby." The years to follow were filled with other names of the day who got their songs in the cylinders and disks that preserved the sounds.

Once Okeh Records recorded a young Mamie Smith, they saw from the sales of Black buyers that money could be made by marketing solely to their demographic. Even as white artists continued releasing covers for the mainstream, if Black consumers had pocket change for a new record, they'd be glad to sell it to them. Let it be noted that this also opened the door for many other ethnic and native musicians to be recorded as the immigration population brought their music to the forefront after the turn of the century.

By the 1920s, "Race Records" took off; by the end of that decade, labels large and small saw the profit in dedicating their own catalogs to Black or "race" music. This inspired talent scouts to comb rural areas and city streets to find the right sound, whether from the poor and unknown migrants to the established nightclub and Black theatre legends.

Even being such innovators, the profits and notoriety from publishing missed many of them. This remained the case late into the music industry's existence, and today the importance of dominating one's own publishing catalogs is only just becoming understood. Back then, it seldom happened; although Black songwriters occupied a respectable portion of the music produced, those songs were freely exploited with little credit or profit given for many until music historians started pulling it apart posthumously.

A partial recap on genres through the years includes:

✓ Negro spirituals couched the soulful melodies and traditional worship of transplanted Africans, allowing Christian conversion to take 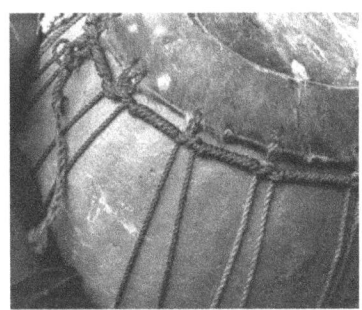 place without losing any of their own identity. The songs could convey pain and suffering as well as use oral traditions and even escape plots as well.

✓ Field hollering, which was tied to the labor, particularly in the south, of tending cotton or tobacco and, on the islands, sugarcane and bananas. The sound was usually a solo cry or holler echoed by the group in chorus. This call and response became the basis for all work songs in the field.

✓ Minstrelsy entered in the nineteenth century, blending a variety of comedic skits, songs, dance, and parody. This was always performed by white people in blackface before the Civil War.

- Blues was given its first start in the North Mississippi delta following the Civil War, the birthing grounds for this genre, when call and response married the guitar.
- Jazz emerged out of New Orleans and Congo Square, where drums had no restrictions and traditional rhythms thrived, as a unique innovation of ethnic groups coming together.
- Ragtime was popular in the 1900s-1920s as an offshoot of marching bands or "jig piano." Almost everybody dug it, white or Black, and it spread quickly around the world.
- Jug band music was just that—homemade instruments like literally jugs, blown in a manner to create a hollowed-out bass sound that, when joined with harmonicas or tambourines, a washtub, and some heavy foot stomping, was quite popular.

- ✓ Big bands would combine sounds with sometimes up to thirteen or more musicians, and the orchestrator would hold the ensemble together as a conductor. It became the swiftest moving vehicle jazz music could take in the 1920s and '30s and launched a lot of major talent, such as Duke Ellington and Count Basie.
- ✓ R&B was a child of the blues and a reflection of the next generation of progressive Black people after the civil rights era began, where soul and more innovative rhythms replaced the heavier themes of straight blues.
- ✓ Country offered more than just banjos and white supremacy themes; it has shown artists both Black and white how to express poverty, hardships, and relationships that any man could relate to. Using instruments derived from African influences, it ironically has been used to mock the people behind the instruments' origins.

- ✓   Modern gospel. Tired of the "sorrow songs" of their grandparents, youth of the Reconstruction period and students among the troupes traveling the globe spreading the music changed the Negro spiritual. They wanted to end the sounds of misery and up the praise; thus, a genre was born.

- ✓   Hip-Hop. The spoken word, oral history delivery, cyphers (joining in a circle as each member chants, speaks, or sings), breakdancing, graffiti art, and the mixing of music into different sounds based on what is on hand (DJs) are all markers of African practices seen today. Started from the African Zulu Nation out of New York, the genre has become the largest-selling one in the world—into the billions.

- ✓   Pop. A more mainstream and often white-dominated (or colorism-driven) sector of the music industry today.

- ✓   Rock. If you have any doubts about this genre's origin, you have only to look to jazz and the blues as well as every credible rock star who ever existed that credited its origins.

- Reggae and other Caribbean styles. The diaspora took the African influence and mixed it with other indigenous cultures as well as that of the colonizers who enslaved them and their cultures. It ends in an exotic blend of music unlike any other in the world.

"Jazz speaks for life," King said. "The blues tell the story of life's difficulties—and, if you think for a moment, you realize that they take the hardest realities of life and put them into music, only to come out with some new hope or sense of triumph. This is triumphant music."
—Dr. Martin Luther King Jr., delivering the opening address to the Berlin Jazz Festival, 1964

CHAPTER SEVEN

BEATS, REVOLUTION & RESISTANCE

The 1950s-'70s protest music painted a picture of current affairs and of what African descendants were still dealing with. The 1960s gave us soulful folk artists like Odetta, an outspoken vocalist bringing the message of equal rights to all. Her music became a foundation for the growing soundtrack backing the burgeoning civil rights movement. She gave a renowned live performance in 1963 during the March on Washington after being introduced by Dr. King himself.

Her albums, such as Odetta and the Blues, One Grain of Sand, It's a Mighty World, and Odetta Sings Dylan, were all iconic examples of resistance music during the 1960s. Another woman whose legendary message-filled music reverberated throughout the sixties was Nina Simone, with songs like "Mississippi Goddamn" in 1964.

The '70s were no less active in musical demonstrations, with Curtis Mayfield's "(Don't Worry) If There's a Hell Below, We're All Going to Go" in 1970 and Marvin Gaye's "What's Going On" in 1971. Both Gaye and Mayfield tried to enlighten us all on the troubled state of race and the violence and poverty tearing apart the inner cities.

Pointing directly to the originating cause of the people's anguish, artists like the O'Jays with their 1973 song, "Ship Ahoy," from the album of the same name, showed us the first trauma set off by the slave trade. Crafted by legendary songwriting team Gamble and Huff, the song was an R&B Billboard chart topper by 1974. The LP's artwork, by James Barkley, depicts African captives stacked as cargo on a ship; the back shows a slave ship floating on water reflecting images of slaves.

Coming in at nine minutes and forty seconds, the extended length offers sounds of being aboard the ship itself, with what appears to be tumultuous waters crashing against the wooden ship's sides in the middle of a storm.

It's an emotionally compelling song that uses extended pauses to grip the listener in the mood of captivity and of suffering, all waiting on the edge of the next note as they sing, "Ship ahoy!" The phrase itself was a call and answer between the sailors of these massive boats passing one another over the great seas.

The O'Jays using it again and again is a call to the listener to acknowledge the events of the slave trade by first seeing those vessels that facilitated it. It begs the listener to answer with their own feelings about such a brutal journey as the Middle Passage.

No music historian today would deny the direct finger-pointing from blues, gospel, ragtime, jazz, rock, and country to those old spirituals, work songs, and slave plantation ring shouts. Whether it's listening to the deep, unmistakably distinct rhythms or understanding the complexity of the use of certain instruments used in the music, you can't miss it.

Our cultural memory is sharp and uninterrupted because of the music, even while Western society likes to play at amnesia when it comes to the contributions of African Americans. By being aware of our history through the music, we can be aware of new degrees of slavery in the twenty-first century.

Modern artists who keep us aware of the impact of that era use the music to teach us that history. From rappers to R&B singers with their fingers on the pulse of current affairs, they still point us back to that fateful Middle Passage and its effects.

These themes come up from Tupac's "Panther Power" to Kanye's "New Slaves," which compare the industrial prison complex to a modern form of slavery. Another rapper,

Nas, referenced it in his 2002 track "Warrior Song," and the emotions are clear in Lauryn Hill's "Black Rage." Yet many in this generation are not hearing the cries from 400 years ago, even through the music. Erasing of the word "slave" from textbooks in Texas to instead read "forced laborer" is just such an erasure.

Haile Gerima's 1993 film Sankofa is translated from an Akan word meaning, "It is not taboo to go back and fetch what you forgot." The title is a poignant reminder of music's true origins. But what about when viewing such realistic depictions is painful or enraging?

These portrayals win even Oscar Awards, such as Denzel Washington's role as a fugitive slave in Glory (1989), a story about an all-Black Civil War unit dealing with the same racism and oppression as their enslaved counterparts. As soldiers fighting a war aimed at abolishing slavery, they reveal the limitations still faced.

Black citizens can only look but so far back before running into forced name changes, forced religion changes, forced interracial births, and suppression of all the things that helped them cope. It might be understood why this generation has no references for looking back to slavery when there is only so much pain to be found there. The music was allowed, and it is one of the safest ways to revisit the pain. Even as it continues to be appropriated, Black music is authentically representative of its people's experiences.

"The Beatles were huge. And the first thing they said when you interviewed them, 'Oh yeah, we grew up on Motown.' They were the first white act to admit they grew up listening to Black music."

—Smokey Robinson

CHAPTER EIGHT

THE BILLION-DOLLAR KEYS

There was an interesting article on Copyblogger about digital sharecropping, which is when content creators do the hard work of making stuff, and then companies like Facebook, Google, Pinterest, and others reap the economic rewards by hosting that free content on their platforms. The author of the article, Sonia Simone, compares the time after the Civil War when sharecropping was practiced to now, how any songs placed on major content platforms stand the same risk when the creator doesn't own it and the giant technology companies make all the profits.

With the story told in R&B, blues, and even rap these days, the lessons of slavery are still around us if we listen. The yoke of it holds back the same community it burdened starting 400 years ago, and today it is a violent one. Mass incarcerations, the parole system, unemployment, opioid and other drug abuses, domestic violence, racial and police profiling, and more act as chains around all people.

By their skills and talents, music and art, Black American ancestors refused to submit to being mere slaves. They also refused to die off or stay ignorant of the ways of the land, and everything they touched flourished. They took a song and added many voices, and with those woke up a sleepy society, and then they colored it and taught it to dance when praising life. The flavors of their traditions feed the world, especially through music.

So, what is Black music today? It's all the genres that beat with the pulse of the Motherland. If we make it and they take it, we always seem to make more. From Elvis Presley to Justin Timberlake, they show us their ability to copy and reflect the music, but just like Black Music Month, celebrated in June in America, shows us, there is a lot to teach about its origins.

That which African ancestors created to survive white domination cannot be destroyed: the spirit and soul of Africa. Bleached, blended, beaten, or oppressed, the African spirit is in the DNA of every culture now, worldwide. Unfortunately, as long as there is capitalism, racism, and some misguided sense of superiority in the world, the exploitation of that in music continues with it.

What can Black music do to liberate a society that is suffering? That is why we keep listening—to find out.

Where is the music industry headed based on its past challenges and on new technology? It now can claim rap as a billion-dollar key to the Black community's wealth. Like the former slaves turned Fisk University Jubilee Singers saved a whole school with their gifts, perhaps the talented artists of today helped save a floundering industry.

The economic and financial model is being looked at much more closely in the music industry than ever before. Right now, the consumer seems to want it all and in no particular order, as we are seeing vinyl sales increase right along with digital sales decreasing, oddly. We are seeing streaming even as the streamers search for profits, and while the industry is not quite sure of where subscription service is going, it is still building up wherever it can. We're in a new phase of transition and undecided on where we want to take this.

Yet, according to the mid-year report by Nielsen Music for 2017, I see some data that really flies off the chart. For albums' single tracks, on-demand audio streaming in 2016 is right at 216 million and 235 million in 2017.

In that chart, the one thing that really sticks out for me is how different genres of music have also been impacted as well. Three years ago, rock was the number one genre of music; by 2017, it's R&B and hip-hop. That's number one at 25 percent, rock at 23 percent, pop at 13 percent, and country at 8 percent. Note that at one point, country was number two.

This indicates a major shift in demand from a consumption standpoint by listeners. Here this study considers what's impacting this.

We can analyze many factors, such as the changing demographics of America and how much racial and social trends impact what we look at on TV and hear in music today. We can observe how independent labels and artists are taking control of their music and its profits and defying major labels, and how different the landscape of Black music looks today as opposed to 50 years ago. We can also view how much this growth, any new advances in platforms for musicians, and the rewards they can reap if allowed into the mainstream are all to be watched—and not just by music lovers but by historians.

Black music, and its people, have come a mighty long way—just as technology has—from the early days of horns and wax. In those archives are lost voices, lost royalties, and even missing credits for who built the beast that is the music industry today.

The business that grew up around Black music from those early field recordings has enslaved artists in newer ways that cannot be imagined. To be ignorant of the history, the technology, the business behind it, and the individuals profiting off it is to repeat a history of suppression.

Let the story be told, just as the songs are sung—loudly and proudly to free the minds and the spirits of any person held captive by circumstance who is seeking the keys to an insuppressible freedom.

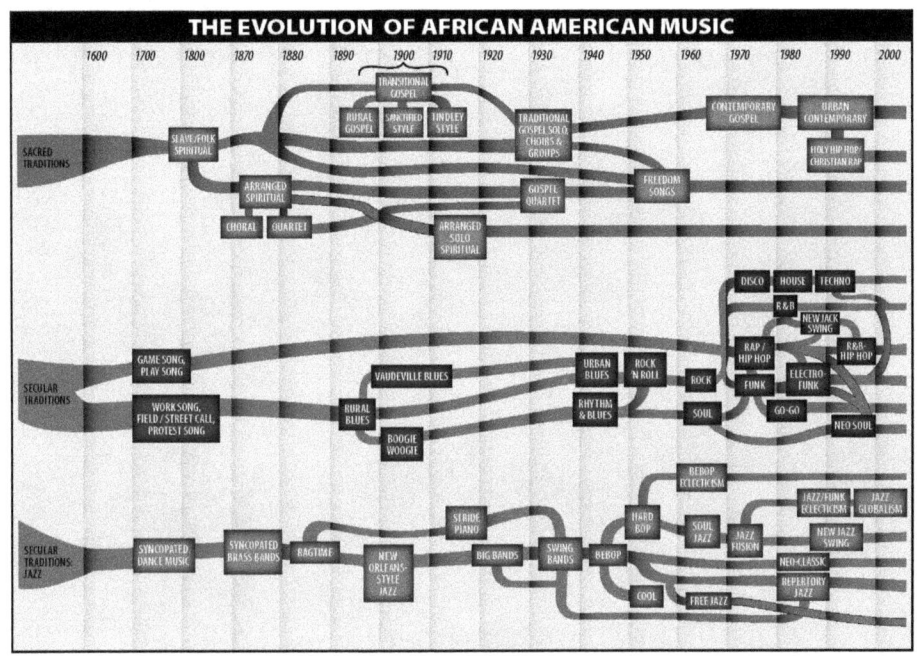

BIBLIOGRAPHY
PRINTED CITATIONS &
DIGITAL REFERENCES

"History of Music." The Method Behind the Music, method-behind-the-music.com/history/history/. Accessed 27 Sept. 2017.

Jaide, Don. "Rasta Livewire." The Place for Africa on the Net, www.africaresource.com/rasta/sesostris-the-great-the-egyptian-hercules/jide-uwechia-the-african-origin-of-the-rnodern-musical-instruments-from-the-fiddle-to-the-guitarro/. Accessed 27 Sept. 2017.

Wilford, John Noble. "Flute's Revised Age Dates the Sound of Music Earlier." The New York Times, 28 May 2012, www.mytimes.com/ZO12/05/29/science/oldest-musical-instruments-are-even-older-than-first-thought.html?mcubz=3. Accessed 27 Sept. 2017.

http://www.harriet-tubman.org/underground-railroad-secret-codes/

https://www.britannica.com/art/African-music#toc5 7067

http://moa.wfu.edu/flles/2012/04/ShakeRattle-Teachers-Guide.pdf

Harriet Tubman, the Moses of her People by Sarah Hopkins Bradford.

http://www.obs.org/wnet/slaverv/experience/education/feature.html

http://www.encyclopedia.com/history/news-wires-white-papers-and-books/history-african-american-music https://www.workers.org/2006/us/music-0209/ http://pathways.thinkportorglsecrets/musicl.cfm

https://www.loc.2ov/item/ihas.200197495/

https://www.si.edu/Spotlight/african-american-music/roots-of-african-american-music

https://thisisafrica.me/lifestyle/drums-allowed-afro-rhythmic-mutations-america/

http://www.africanamericanrnusicnc.com/about-the-music/music-stjles/

"African Americans at Jamestown." National Parks Service, US Department of the Interior, www.nps.gov/jame/learn/historyculture/african-americans-at-jamestown.htm.

History.com, A&E Television Networks, www.history.com/topics/black-history.

"Songs of the Underground Railroad." Harriet Tubman, www.harriet-tubman.org/songs-of-the-underground-railroad/.

https://prezi.com/5xpz2noz_3qw/how-slavery-affected-music/ http://www.pbs.org/wnet/slavery/experience/education/history.html

http://www.encyclopedia.com/history/news-wires-white-papers-and-books/history-african-american-music https://www.ethnomusicologyreview.ucla.edu/content/akonting-history

Shmoop Editorial Team. "Race in Country Music History." Shmoop. Shmoop University, Inc., 11 Nov. 2008. Web. 2 Jun. 2018.

"Did We Sell Each Other Into Slavery: Misconceptions About the African Involvement in the Slave Trade." HuffPost - Breaking News, US and World News I HuffPost. Web. http://www.huffingtonpost.com/dwayne-wong-omowalelmyths-and-misconceptions-1_b_96 37798.html

Howe (1864), Refugees from Slavery in Canada West, pp. 70-71

Kelley, James. Song, Story, or History: Resisting Claims of a Coded Message in the African American Spiritual "Follow the Drinking Gourd." The Journal of Popular American Culture 41.2 (April 2008): 262-80.

The Middle Passage: The Abolition of Slavery Project." The Abolition of Slavery Project. Web. <http://abolition.e2bn.org/slavery44.html>.

The history of the transatlantic slave trade - International Slavery Museum, Liverpool museums." National Museums Liverpool. Web. <http://www.liverpoolmuseums.org.uk/ism/slavery/index.aspx>.

An Encyclopedia of African American Christian Heritage by Marvin Andrew McMickle Judson Press, Copyright 2002 ISBN 0-817014-02-0.

"What part of Africa did most slaves come from? - Ask History." HISTORY I Watch Full Episodes of Your Favorite Shows. Web. http://www.history.com/news/ask-history/what-part-of-africa-di d-most-slaves-come-from.

Sylviane Diouf, Servants of Allah: African Muslims Enslaved in the Americas (NYU Press, 2013).

Black Then I Discovering Our History. Web. <http://blackthen.com/dancing-the-slaves-a-look-into-the-inhumane-treatment-of-africans-aboard-slave-ships/>.

Brooks, Tim. The Columbia Master Book Discography, Volume I. Westport: Greenwood, 1999.

Lost Sounds: Blacks and the Birth of the Recording Industry, 1890-1919.

Urbana: University of Illinois Press, 2004.

Gaisberg, Frederick William. The Music Goes Round. New York: The Macmillan Company, 1942.

Wexler, Jerry; Ritz, David (1993). Rhythm and the Blues: A Life in American Music. New York: Alfred A. Knopf. ISBN 0-224-03963-6.

Kenney, William Howland. Recorded Music in American Life. New York: Oxford University Press, 1999.

Koenigsberg, Allen. Edison Cylinder Records, 1889-1912. New York: Stellar Productions, 1969.

Millard, Andre. America on Record: A History of Recorded Sound. New York: Cambridge University Press, 1995.

Rust, Brian A. L. Jazz Records 1897-1842. New Rochelle: Arlington House, 1978.

Ramsey, Guthrie P., Jr. (2003). Race Music: Black Cultures from Bebop to Hip-Hop. Music of the African Diaspora, 7. Berkeley and London: University of California Press; Chicago, Illinois: Center for Black Music Research, Columbia College. ISBN 0-520-21048-4.

Rust, Brian A. L., and Allen G. Debus. The Complete Entertainment Discography from 1897 to 1942. New York: Da Capo Press, 1989.

Spottswood, Richard K. Ethnic Music on Records. Urbana: University of Illinois Press, 1990.

http://archive.is/gHbHg WAYS OF LIFE // Part 1: Original Affluence

Jazz Roots http://www.jass.com/External

Recording Pioneer George W. Johnson http://www.npr.org/templates/story/story.php?storyId=5224572 External

Mainspring Press http://www.mainspringpress.com/victorsales.htmlExternal

http://revealinghistories.org.uk/legacies-stereotypes-racism-and-the-civil-rights-movement/articles/legacies-of-slavery-dance.html

http://www.africandiasporatourism.com/index.php/index.php?option=com_content&view=article&id=383:underground-railroad-escape-to-the-elgin-settlement&catid=93:culture-3&Itemid=134

Black Musicians from Slavery to Freedom: An Exploration of an African American Folk Elite and Cultural Continuity in the Nineteenth-Century Rural South. By Paul A. Cimbala.

George, Nelson (June 26, 1982). "Black Music Charts: What's in a Name?" Billboard. p. 10.

Joshua Clark Davis wrote in For the Records: How African American Consumers and Music Retailers Created Commercial Public Space in the 1960s and 1970s South," Southern Cultures, Winter 2011.

Foreman, Ronald C. Jr. (1969). Jazz and Race Records, 1920–32. University Microfilms International.

Millard, Andre (2013). Cassette Tape (2.1 ed.). St. James Encyclopedia of Popular Culture. p. 529. https://entertainment.slashdot.org/story/13/02/24/1822252/napster-the-day-the-music-was-set-free.

July 12, 2000 BBC News, MP3 Sites Accused of Music 'Hijack' http://news.bbc.co.uk/2/hi/americas/829668.stm.

SONY CHAIRMAN NIXES ANY DEAL WITH NAPSTER By Allyson Lieberman December 22, 2000 https://nypost.com/2000/12/22/sony-chairman-nixes-any-deal-with-napster/.

Nielsen US MUSIC MID-YEAR REPORT 2017

ENTERTAINMENT | 07-05-2017 Millennials' Preferences Are Disrupting Music Business

By Michelle Borré and Daryl Armstrong

March 8, 2017

https://www.barrons.com/articles/sponsored/millennials-preferences-are-disrupting-music-business-1488481041?tesla=y

https://www.marketingweek.com/2015/10/21/how-streaming-can-transform-music-marketing/

Recommended Listening

Billie Holiday, "Travelin Light"

Marvin Gaye, "What's Going On"

The O'Jays, "Ships Ahoy"

Curtis Mayfield, "(Don't Worry) If There's a Hell Below, We're All Going to Go"

Tupac, "Panther Power"

Brad Paisley feat. LL Cool J, "Accidental Racist"

ABOUT THE AUTHOR

Author, professor, lecturer, motivational speaker, music executive, artist manager, entrepreneur, fighter, and cancer survivor would be the words used to sum up the life and career of Mathew Knowles.

Dr. Knowles possesses an MBA in Strategic Planning and Organizational Culture and a Ph.D in Business Administration. Knowles recently attended Harvard's Professional Development courses in ethical leadership as well as developing cultural intelligence. He currently holds a professorship at Point Blank Music School – Los Angeles, University of Houston, Prairie View A&M University, and The Art Institute.

As a pioneer for African American success in the corporate world, Knowles' corporate career includes sales and marketing at Xerox Medical Systems, Phillips Medical System, and Johnson & Johnson. He has sold over 450 million records worldwide, having architected the careers of Destiny's Child, Beyonce, and Solange, to name a few, and has worked with legends such as Chaka Kahn, O'Jays, Earth, Wind & Fire, and many others.

www.ingramcontent.com/pod-product-compliance
Lightning Source LLC
Chambersburg PA
CBHW060641150426
42811CB00078B/2241/J